SEX AND THE CATHOLIC FEMINIST

SUE ELLEN BROWDER

Sex and the Catholic Feminist

New Choices for a New Generation

IGNATIUS PRESS
San Francisco

AUGUSTINE INSTITUTE
Greenwood Village, CO

Cover Design: Christina Gray

© 2020 by Ignatius Press, San Francisco, and
the Augustine Institute, Greenwood Village, CO
All rights reserved.
ISBN 978-1-950939-03-9
Library of Congress Control Number 2020930301
Printed in Canada ∞

This work is dedicated to and placed
under the protection of the Mother of God,
our leader in battle.

The difficulty lies not so much in developing new ideas as in escaping from old ones.

—John Maynard Keynes

The Truth is like a lion. You don't have to defend it. Let it loose. It will defend itself.

—Saint Augustine

CONTENTS

INTRODUCTION

It's Time to Reclaim the F-Word
(No, Not That One!)

It may have begun much earlier, but my conversion of heart from being a pro-choice feminist to a pro-life feminist began to crystallize on Saturday, January 24, 2009, in San Francisco on the Golden Gate Bridge. My dear friend Robin Carter, who had endured the scars and ravages of three abortions, had courageously vowed to be "silent no more" and was preparing to tell her intimate story to the thousands of people who were pouring into the city for the West Coast Walk for Life. She'd asked me to come along with her for moral support.

On that cloudy day, as we drove across the Golden Gate Bridge, Robin fought off a panic attack as she told me about her first abortion. I'll spare you all the grisly details of her depersonalizing meat-market experience. But after the ordeal, when she was crying while being wheeled from the operating room, one Planned Parenthood worker turned to another and sneered. "This one's crying for her mother."

Once we arrived in San Francisco, the Walk for Life was like no other protest I'd ever witnessed. Here were literally thousands of women, men, and children—Black, Caucasian, Hispanic, Asian, Native American, *everyone*—marching peacefully together side by side with one common aim: to end legalized abortion on demand in America. Many were singing, chanting, and praying. A spirit of joy filled the air. I sensed a vibrant energy and a unity of minds and hearts I'd previously witnessed only sometimes in church. This wasn't a political protest as most people know it, and it certainly wasn't a riot. Although it would take years for me to be able to articulate what I was seeing, this was liturgy outside liturgy. This was a loving community with open arms stretched out to all persons. This was contemplative prayer in action.

As I walked along with this crowd of thirty thousand strangers united as one body in an army of love, the thought (or was it a prayer?) suddenly came to me: "O my God, the media have completely missed this story, and I'm one of those who have missed it." With new eyes, I suddenly saw that the abortion story in our nation is not about *me* vs. *you*, what *I* want vs. what *you* want. It's not even about left vs. right, liberal vs. conservative, or Democrat vs. Republican. The story America needs to hear is about *all* of us working in harmony, united in love—*together*. Viewing the pro-life phenomenon from the outside as an observer (as I'd previously viewed it) was a radically different experience from the beauty of the story now unfolding around me as a participant. It was as if I'd been standing outside alone on a cold rainy night and had suddenly walked through a door into a land of wonder filled with flowers, music, and sunshine.

After my friend Robin gave her testimony on the Silent No More stage, Father Frank Pavone (national director of Priests for Life) stepped up to the microphone and addressed the crowd. His speech was inspired, but as I write this ten years later, I can clearly recall only six words that he said. As I stood on the ground in front of the stage looking up at Father Frank, he looked down, seemingly straight at me, and pointedly asked, "What are *you* going to do?"

I was flabbergasted. Until that moment, I had been thinking about writing a history of the women's movement; now I realized I *had* to write it. I had to record how the feminist movement (with its unifying cries for fair treatment of women in academia and the workforce) and the sexual revolution (with its divisive demands for abortion and contraception) got joined together, as I had witnessed the story unfold and as God had opened my eyes to see it. The story you're about to read (along with my previous book *Subverted: How I Helped the Sexual Revolution Hijack the Women's Movement*) is my answer to Father Frank's question.

Of course, to many ears, the very concept of pro-life feminism sounds scandalous. Since publishing *Subverted*, I've given talks to many groups across the country, from San Francisco to Boston, and I frequently begin by asking this question: "How many of you are pro-life?" Since I'm talking to audiences made up mostly of Christians, nearly everyone raises a hand. Then I ask: "How many are feminists?" All hands, except one or two, go down. Many people consider the idea that you can be both pro-life *and* a feminist to be an unthinkable contradiction. In some crowds, this thought raises so many hackles that I've begun, somewhat tongue-in-cheek, to call "feminism" the new F-word.

You can't be a feminist and believe in God, right? You certainly can't be a feminist, love marriage, and be a happy, full-time mom, can you? Well, at least that's the story our culture usually tells. What's popularly called "feminism" in our culture is associated with so much anger, political outrage, resentment, and pain that many women and men understandably want nothing to do with it.

Yet Pope Saint John Paul II urged Catholics not to reject feminism entirely nor to embrace it entirely, but to embody a "new feminism," a radical view of women's dignity that takes the genuine human yearnings hidden within the old feminism, lifts them up to a higher dimension, and points the way forward for women in today's rapidly changing world.[1] In private audiences, the joyful saint even took to calling himself "il Papa feminista"[2]— "the feminist Pope"!

What a strange notion. A *new* feminism? Whatever could he have meant by that? He certainly wasn't talking about women becoming priests. He made that crystal clear in his 1994 apostolic letter on priestly ordination.[3] Nor was he urging Catholic women to take to the streets and start angrily waving placards and screaming slogans. Nor could he have been urging us to create just another political action plan. On the one hand, as responsible citizens, we all need to vote and do whatever we can to promote political and social justice. And yet, on the other hand (as John Paul knew perhaps better than most), no political system will ever provide the ultimate answers to women's deepest questions, and no utopian plan—whether it's feminism, Communism, or any other "-ism"—will ever turn this world into an earthly paradise.

On the contrary, the painfully outdated sort of feminism I once believed in and actively promoted has gone hand in hand, not with a feminine utopia, but with contemporary turmoil, including a divorce epidemic, millions of aborted babies, a multibillion-dollar porn industry, widespread gender confusion, and a free-for-all sexual culture on high school and college campuses that makes it easy for a young woman to say yes to sex but almost impossible for her to say no. The #MeToo Movement has unveiled the appalling reality that for some men "You've come a long way, baby," means "Yippee! You're liberated. Now I can have sex with you whenever I please."

And yet, in the midst of all this ... a *new* pro-life Catholic feminism? The very concept seems self-contradictory. However are we to find such a thing?

Well, for years while I was writing articles for *Cosmopolitan* and other women's magazines in the 1970s through the 1990s, I was a pro-abortion feminist. I didn't become Catholic until I was fifty-seven. As a journalist and freelance writer, I was able to witness, at least in part, how we ended up where we are today. And I'd suggest we can resolve the paradox and begin to find this new feminism by digging down to the roots of the old feminism to see where it went right and where it went wrong. My goal in this little book is not to write a comprehensive global history of feminism (which would require many thousands of pages), but simply to follow one golden thread of feminism in America—the pro-life thread—to show why it has been ignored by the media and left out of the public conversation for fifty years.

In the 1970s, '80s, and '90s, when I was writing articles for *Cosmopolitan* and *New Woman*,* and even for years after that, I sincerely believed the type of feminism that included "sexual liberation" (along with its concomitant demands for abortion and contraception) was the path to women's freedom. I didn't even think to question this belief. It seemed self-evident to me. In 1992, when I was a contributing editor at *New Woman*, I even helped research and write a little book titled *How to Make the World a Better Place for Women in Five Minutes a Day*, which included a number of simple steps I sincerely believed any allegedly "smart" woman could—and should—take to save the abortion right in America.[4]

---

* This popular woman's magazine with a feminist slant had a circulation of over one million and folded in 1999 (it is not to be confused with a magazine of the same name published in India).

Even after I became serious about my Christian faith, first as an Episcopalian and then as a Catholic, I still managed to cling to my conviction that "reproductive rights" were unalloyed goods for women. In my mind, the Catholic Church was right about God, but when it came to women's rights, the stuffy old Church "just didn't get it." In my pride, I was secretly saying that when it came to women's rights *God* "just didn't get it." But I didn't realize that's what I was saying.

Still, I've been an investigative reporter all my adult life. I'm used to listening to people so I can hear their stories, even if I personally think their point of view is outrageous or wrong. When working for women's magazines in New York City, I was surrounded by ambitious editors and writers who thought about feminism the same way I did—as a way for a woman to control her life and to get ahead in the world. But after I moved to the northern California redwood country, for the first time I began listening to pro-life women on the other side of the cultural divide. The more deeply I listened, the more I began to sense that these pro-life women disagreed with me not because they had a *smaller* vision of reality than I did but because they saw a *bigger* picture. These strong, intelligent women were not simply conformists following the crowd, as I'd always been told. They were thinking seriously for themselves—but in an entirely new way, a way of thinking radically different from the way I'd been taught to think all my life. They had a broader, less fragile, and more resilient sense of self than many women I knew. Life's difficulties didn't unduly upset them. They taught me that "pro-life" is about far more than abortion and contraception. It's about loving, respecting, nurturing, and supporting all human life, no matter what the age, size, or state of development. The weakest humans, they said, deserve not the least but the *most* care. Fascinated and curious, I began to dig deeper.

Slowly, as I began to leave my old ways of thinking behind, I came to see that it's not feminism *per se* that's contrary to the Judeo-Christian worldview. What pro-life women oppose is not feminism itself, but *the false joining of feminism with the sexual revolution.* It's not feminism (the call for women to be treated with equal dignity and respect) that's contrary to Judeo-Christian values. What's contrary to these values is the core of what occurred through the sexual revolution: reducing a woman's personhood to her sex organs, sexual desirability, and sexual desires, denying motherhood, rejecting marriage, discarding the family, and then pretending this reduction of her personhood somehow augments her freedom.

I came to understand that feminism has led to so much polarization in our society not because Americans disagree over the fundamental issues (dignity and respect for all women everywhere) but at least in part because so many media people like me can't seem to get their story straight, and they keep perpetuating fantasies that keep women tied up in knots. The most destructive, divisive, media-perpetuated fantasy is the delusion that anything-goes sex with no commitment from the man somehow "liberates" a woman, enabling her to become fully herself. Anytime you desacralize human sexuality, turning it away from love and into a pursuit of pleasure or power, everyone loses. What began as a revolution for sexual freedom has disintegrated into a degrading parody of freedom that has left many women and men disenchanted, angry, wounded, and lonely.

Listening for years to both the pro-choice and the pro-life sides of women's stories has convinced me that the pro-life movement—precisely *because* it defends strong relationships within marriage and the family and rejects the sexual revolution's divisive demands for casual sex, abortion, and other imagined sexual "freedoms"—represents *the authentic women's movement of the twenty-first century.* Further, I'm convinced that pro-life family feminism, already well-organized at the grassroots level, will be unstoppable in the years ahead if all women and men— Democrats and Republicans alike—stop fighting, pull together, and recognize we're all working toward the same goals: for genuine respect and dignity for all women, men, and children, rich or poor, of all ages and stages of life, of all races, in America and around the globe.

My hope is that some thoughts presented here will spark a new conversation and help heal one of the deepest political divisions in our nation. Our warring world desperately needs women and men who are at interior peace with themselves to bring peace to our nation and to comfort and cultivate courage in others. If you're pro-life but don't see yourself as a feminist, perhaps you will come to see why you're *already* a feminist even if you presently reject the F-word. If you're pro-choice, perhaps the ideas presented here will help you see why you keep facing so much opposition. If you already consider yourself a pro-life feminist, maybe this little book will help further your thoughts on the subject. In our increasingly fragmented world, we desperately need to find ways to set aside our political differences so we can move forward hand in hand. This book is meant to be not a stick but an olive branch.

Unfortunately, one thing that keeps women and men so divided in our nation is the word "feminism" itself. Because some of the loudest feminist voices in the public square have been so hostile toward men, motherhood, marriage, the family, and the Church, many pro-life Christians believe this particular F-word is so polluted that it can never be purified. Since feminism is one of those "-isms" invented by flawed humans, some people maintain it won't last. An empty word stripped of all meaning, it will make a noise for a while; then it will be heard no more.

There's much truth in this viewpoint, and I deeply respect this opinion. Even feminist historians have been pronouncing feminism dead for thirty years.[5] But the noise of feminism and the cry for women's dignity have not gone away. Women are still marching in the streets and speaking out in the public square. Why? I think it's because on some level, with an awareness that lies deep in their hearts, we women know that what our foremothers began fighting for in the 1800s—true respect for the dignity of a woman's full *personhood* in both the public and private spheres of life—has not yet been achieved.

What's more, as Christians, we need to forgive those we perceive to be our enemies, because only when we see the good in them will we begin to see the light. Christ makes *all* things new, even the deep human yearnings hidden at the roots of feminism.

In fact, the core concepts originally conveyed by the word "feminism" (respect for the dignity of all women everywhere) grew out of a Christian worldview. But along the way, the word "feminism"—and the core concepts it once conveyed—became subverted and corrupted.

Abuse of language, twentieth-century philosopher Joseph Pieper observed, is abuse of power. Words matter because language frames our thoughts. If we allow our words to become twisted and corrupted by the selfish purposes of others, we will eventually find the thoughts of many around us corrupted.

With feminism, this has already happened. Sex profiteers (who rake in billions of dollars by using women's naked or half-clad bodies to capture consumer attention) have stolen feminism and are using it to sell young women everything from abortion to "girl power" T-shirts, "power woman" perfume, and Spanx "women's power" panties. Everywhere we turn, cynical marketers are using feminism and the idea of sex as "power" to sell women and girls on an attitude that's the exact opposite of love and can deeply damage their relationships, physical health, and mental well-being.

The old, outdated, pro-choice form of feminism, the kind I promoted for more than twenty years when I was freelancing for *Cosmo* and other women's magazines, promises women happiness, freedom, and self-actualization. That's the dream. Yet when women try to live out this dream in real life, it frequently backfires on those who take it most seriously. As one pro-choice feminist who admitted she had "virtually no close female friends" sadly confessed, "Sometimes it seemed that feminism was the only thing that mattered in my life. And to be honest, it wasn't making my life very happy. I felt disenfranchised, marginalized, and perpetually disappointed."[6]

As a matter of truth and justice, rather than abandon the fight for freedom and dignity that rightfully belongs to us, I think we as Christians need to rise above what the media has traditionally called "feminism" (the pro-choice sort) and restore it to its proper meaning if for no other reason than to save women and girls—along with men and boys—who have been confused and deceived by what the loudest voices in our culture are saying.

Women's bodies have now been largely reduced to commodities in the public square, and only the most confident, best educated, and least desperate young women are able to dodge all the sexual bullets flying about their heads. By shunning the "feminist" label as Christians, we're allowing sex-revolution propagandists (advertisers, marketers, and other sex profiteers) to control the public story and to claim *they're* the cool ones standing up for women and girls while Christians are just a bunch of old fuddy-duddies stuck in the Dark Ages.

Loving, intelligent men—particularly fathers—who firmly stand up against this sexualized feminist onslaught are too often dismissed as sexist tyrants and bullies. If a true, authentic vision for feminine freedom is ever to be articulated in our society, intelligent pro-life Christians are the ones who will have to stand up and speak out. The ball is in our court. We each have a responsibility to decide what we will do at this critical moment in history. So let's not tie ourselves up in knots over a word. There's too much at stake. Whatever your thoughts may be about the F-word, let's all agree on one thing. Love, motherhood, marriage, and relationships matter.

It's time to take back our story.

I

REMEMBERING OUR STORY

There's a strong sense even among secular people in our society that the old feminism veered offtrack somewhere along the way. On the one hand, women are earning more college degrees than men and more women are going to law school. Far more women than ever before in U.S. history are being elected to city councils, state legislatures, and Congress. Yet on the other hand, as the #MeToo Movement has clearly revealed, many women and girls are still treated like pleasure-giving sex objects, and they've been intimidated into silence for decades.

"We live in a very pornographic age where women are both worshipped as goddesses and yet, ironically, only used and abused for their anatomy and physical beauty," observes Father Donald Calloway, a Marian priest. "At one and the same time, the media claim to fight for the rights of women, yet they also ardently promote and defend the abuse of women through the smut of pornography that is daily displayed in their sitcoms and television programs. It's schizophrenic!"[1]

What's going on?

We're often told there's a "war on women." Unfortunately, the media have once again missed the most important element of the story. Twentieth-century British Broadcasting Corporation (BBC) journalist Malcolm

Muggeridge once wryly quipped that a strange thing he'd discovered in his many years in the business of news gathering and news presentation was "that, by some infallible process, media people almost always manage to miss the most important thing."[2] In this case, the most important thing we media people have missed is that the real war is not *on* women but *between* women.

The real battle is over *personhood* and what it means to be a person. It's a conflict between strong, intelligent, liberated women, on the one hand, who put the quest for sex, career, money, power, and other self-gratifying pleasures *first* in an attempt to *create their own identities*, versus strong, intelligent, liberated women, on the other hand, who believe *their identities are given to them by God* and the path to human wholeness is found primarily through self-giving love for God and others. For fifty years, we as Americans have been embroiled in a bitterly polarized cultural war *between* women that is tearing our nation apart.

And now the #MeToo Movement has plainly unveiled the fact that no matter how far women have come in our struggle for equal dignity and respect, we still have a long way to go.

This book is not meant to divide strong women once again into separate camps by labeling some women as "wrong" and "bad" and others as "righteous" and "good." Rather, it's my hope that once you see how we got where we are today, the insights you gain as a result of knowing the truth will help heal the tragic divisions between women and men that have so wounded our nation.

It's precisely in times of historical upheaval like this, when the answers from the past no longer satisfy and new questions emerge, that we need to pause and reflect upon history. If you're young, it's your generation's task to question the meanings and values handed down to you by my generation. Despite Americans' political differences, the need to defend the freedom and dignity of all persons is one value on which all people of goodwill can agree. The reduction of a woman's full personhood to her sexual desirability and sexual desires is the real injustice we're fighting. So let's begin to unravel the tangled knots in which the old, outmoded feminism is trapped by going back a century to that era when pro-life feminists won women the right to vote.

Pro-Life Christians Fight for the Vote

Modern feminism, largely because of its post-1967 advocacy for abortion and contraception and its later attacks on "patriarchy" and the family, has come to be seen by many people to be antiman and antifamily. But this wasn't always the case. On the contrary, our culture has forgotten that many first-wave feminists who won women the right to vote were Christians who opposed abortion, loved men, championed the family, and saw their hard work as a mission grounded in their faith.

One early pro-life Christian feminist was suffragist Alice Paul, who spearheaded the campaign leading to the passage of the U.S. Constitution's Nineteenth Amendment, giving women the right to vote. Born in 1885 on a small farm in New Jersey, Alice stated that her work on behalf of women was firmly rooted in her upbringing among Quakers, who believed men and women have equal dignity in the eyes of God. "When the Quakers were founded in England in the 1600s," Alice told *American Heritage* magazine, "one of their principles was and is equality of the sexes. So I never had any other idea.... The principle was always there."[3] At a time in our nation when Americans rarely went to college and fewer than five hundred Ph.D. degrees were awarded annually, Alice received a master's degree and Ph.D. in sociology from the University of Pennsylvania and went on to earn not one but three law degrees. But she gave up the easy life of a scholar and the aristocratic world of a cultured, prosperous Quaker family for what one of her co-suffragists called "the rigors of ceaseless drudgery and frequent imprisonment."[4] Under her inspired leadership, the women's suffrage movement (which was launched in the 1800s but had gone dormant) sprang back to life. Donations to two organizations she chaired shot up from $10 in 1912 to $27,000 in 1913.[5]

In 1913, Alice and her dear friend Lucy Burns (a Vasser-educated Irish Catholic from Brooklyn who did postgraduate work at Yale and the universities of Bonn, Berlin, and Oxford) worked together to form the Congressional Union for Woman Suffrage to fight for the vote. In 1916, they broke away from the Congressional Union and formed the National Woman's Party.

When Alice, Lucy, and their "silent sentinels" picketed the White House for months to demand that President Woodrow Wilson (a Democrat) speak up for women's right to vote, they and forty other women were illegally arrested and thrown into a disease-infested prison workhouse where they were obliged to strip naked, given "hideous prison clothes" of bluish-gray ticking,[6] and fed bowls of rancid soup in which worms were floating.[7] Lucy—a forgotten hero of the movement—led most of the picket demonstrations and served more time in jail than any other suffragist in America.[8]

Shortly after their arrival in the workhouse, as suffrage attorney Doris Stevens recalled in her book *Jailed for Freedom*, the women were called one by one into the warden's office. One exchange with Doris's female interrogator went like this:

"What religion to you profess?"

"Christian."

"What religion do you profess?" in a higher pitched voice.

I did not clearly comprehend. "Do you mean 'Am I a Catholic or a Protestant?' I am a Christian."

But it was of no avail. She wrote down, "None."

I protested. "That is not accurate. I insist that I am a Christian, or at least I *try* to be one."

"You must learn to be polite," she retorted almost fiercely, and I returned to the sewing room.[9]

The tubs in which the suffragists were forced to bathe were located in a room housing a syphilitic female inmate with one leg (the other one having been cut off when it was so rotted it was alive with maggots).[10] Yet refusing to despair, these indomitable women kept their spirits up with evening songs and prayers. "Mary Winsor of Haverford, Pennsylvania, was the master prayer-maker," Stevens recalled. "One night it was a Baptist prayer, another a Methodist, and still another a stern Presbyterian prayer."[11]

As a final protest against unjust imprisonment and increasingly long sentences, Alice, Lucy, and others began to fast and were force-fed by having to lie prone while guards rammed a pipe down their throats into their stomachs, a brutality that left them faint and vomiting.

Despite all this, Alice's fortitude and serene peace of mind were unshakable. After being confined in solitary for weeks, she was placed in a psychiatric ward and threatened with incarceration in an insane asylum—an intimidating prospect for anyone. Yet the doctor examining her observed in his notes, "I felt myself in the presence of an unusually gifted personality. . . . She was wonderfully alert and keen ... possessed of an absolute conviction of her cause ... with industry and courage." He praised the "most admirable, coherent, logical and forceful way"[12] in which Alice discussed with him the purpose of the women's suffrage campaign. Contrary to popular feminist opinion, biblical *meekness* is not weakness, but strength wisely withheld. One must be truly strong to be gentle. A fortress of resilience, Alice was both.

When Alice was first unjustly sentenced to seven months in jail for picketing the White House, both men and women were saying, "This is terrible! A seven-month sentence is impossible. You must stop! You can't keep this up!"

Yet Doris recalled, "With an unmistakable note of triumph in her voice Miss Paul would answer, 'Yes, it is terrible for us, but not nearly so terrible as for the government. The Administration has fired its heaviest gun. From now on we shall win and they will lose.'"[13] And she was right.

The invincible Alice Paul was a courageous role model for pro-life Christian feminists everywhere. With her strength calmly anchored in her relationship with the Father, the Son, and the Holy Spirit, she wasn't the least afraid to speak up clearly and express her convictions boldly. Now please don't get me wrong. I'm not saying *all* the early feminists were Christians. They certainly were not. But neither was the Christian faith opposed to the goals of the first-wave feminist movement.

After fighting with others to win women the right to vote, Alice went on to draft the Equal Rights Amendment (ERA). Known for her unflinching fearlessness in the face of opposition, Alice saw abortion as the ultimate in the exploitation of women[14] and said when women call for abortion, it "gets the men all mixed up."[15] (As we shall see in chapters 4 and 5, however, not *all* the men were mixed up over abortion. Some knew *exactly* what they were doing.)

When the ERA faced bitter opposition in the 1970s, Alice also blamed liberal feminists' demands for abortion for what she predicted would soon be the amendment's defeat.[16] Of course, abortion certainly wasn't the only reason for the ERA's defeat.[17] But Alice's prediction that the amendment would go up in smoke did come true; five years after her death, the ERA failed to be ratified by two-thirds of the states.

In her defense of the invisible bond of love between unborn babies and their mothers, Alice Paul was far from alone. As retired Villanova University law professor Joseph Dellapenna observed in his masterful 1,283-page tome, *Dispelling the Myths of Abortion History,*

> Margaret Sanger, famous as the founder of the birth control movement, consistently and repeatedly condemned abortion as murder. Dr. Marie Stopes, who played a similar role in England, also condemned abortion as murder. As late as 1960, Dr. Mary Calderone, the medical director of Planned Parenthood and later one of the strongest supporters of the supposed freedom to abort, described abortion as "the taking of a life." In short, until quite recently most feminists were strong opponents of abortion, and the farther back one goes in time the more nearly unanimous feminists become in their hostility to abortion.[18]

So why, Professor Dellapenna asked, do so many pro-abortion historians (including Stanford University's James Mohr and the late NARAL attorney Cyril Chestnut Means) "seem incapable of realizing that until recently even the most militant feminists considered abortion an abominable crime against nature and against women, a crime that society should prohibit and attempt to stamp out"? Dellapenna concludes that historical revisionists have crafted a new history of abortion "for which there is no evidence except the historian's intuition."[19]

Summing up the facts of history, Eastern Orthodox Christian Frederica Mathewes-Green observed in the *Tampa Tribune*: "For over a hundred years, feminists have warned us that abortion is a form of oppression and violence against women and children. They called it 'child-murder' (Susan B. Anthony), 'degrading to women' (Elizabeth Cady Stanton), 'most barbaric' (Margaret Sanger)*.... How have we lost this wisdom?"[20] It's my hope that by the time you finish reading this little book you'll be able to answer this question.

After women won the right to vote in 1920, there was widespread belief that the political fight for women's liberation in the U.S. was over. Feminism virtually disappeared from the public stage as Americans struggled during the Great Depression to put food on the table and then rallied to fight World War II. But in the 1950s and '60s, prosperity returned, and consumerism exploded. Whether it was a microwave oven, a super floor waxer, or that amazing newfangled device called a TV, America was swept up in the consumerist quest for possessions and status. That's when Betty Friedan appeared on the scene and launched the second-wave feminist movement with her book *The Feminine Mystique*.

---

* One forgotten piece of history is that Planned Parenthood founder Margaret Sanger—who thought of herself as a feminist—went to her death bed *opposing abortion*, and it was only after Dr. Alan Guttmacher, a man, took over Planned Parenthood that the organization began in 1968 to advocate the repeal of all abortion laws.

Misnaming "The Problem That Had No Name"

In a survey she'd been asked to conduct for her Smith College class reunion, Betty Friedan discovered that all this upscale consumerism was not making women happy.[21] In the 1950s, Betty was married with three children, living in a well-appointed home in the suburbs. But her unhappy marriage felt like a prison, and she longed to escape.

Betty's Smith College survey revealed that many other educated women her age were also struggling with a sad sense of emptiness. Women reported inexplicable crying jags, anger attacks, and "a strange feeling of desperation." They were flocking to psychiatrists by the thousands and "taking tranquilizers like cough drops." Some women described "great bleeding blisters" that broke out on their hands and arms. One woman said, "You wake up in the morning and you feel as if there's no point in going on another day like this. So you take a tranquilizer because it makes you not care so much that it's pointless."

Betty wrote, "Each suburban wife struggled with it alone. As she made the beds, shopped for groceries, matched slipcover material, ate peanut butter sandwiches with her children, chauffeured Cub Scouts and Brownies, lay beside her husband at night—she was afraid to ask even of herself the silent question—'Is this all?'"[22]

In many ways, these well-educated, upper-middle-class, middle-aged women in their tidy suburban homes were living the American Dream. And yet despite their apparent affluence, their interior lives were in chaos. Why were they so depressed, anxious, and unhappy? They seemed to be asking themselves not "What do I need to live?" but "What am I living *for*?" Were they trying to fill the God-sized hole in their hearts with things other than God, and did their unhappiness spring from the natural human hunger to find a deeper meaning in their lives? Were they spiritually impoverished and, in the words of Catholic feminist Edith Stein (St. Teresa Benedicta of the Cross), "yearning to be raised above their narrow, day-to-day existence into the realm of higher being"?[23] Such deeper questions at least deserved to be asked. For to free ourselves from interior chaos, observed Alexander Elchaninov in *Diary of a Russian Priest*, we must recognize objective order.[24]

But Betty, who would later sign a public document† stating that she didn't believe in the objective order of a loving God who hears and answers our prayers, had no spiritual vocabulary with which to ask such questions. Blind to the possibility these women might be struggling with any number of psychological, physical, and spiritual problems, she concluded they were all suffering from what she dubbed "the problem that had no name." She then proceeded to name (or, rather, to oversimplify and *misname*) the problem. She called it *The Feminine Mystique*, which she defined as the deeply engrained cultural belief that the only path to feminine fulfillment was to be "just a housewife."

For Betty, the solution to the nameless problem was work. "The only way for a woman, as for a man, to find herself, to know herself as a person, is by creative work of her own," Betty wrote. "There is no other way."[25] She

---

†The document she signed was the Humanist Manifesto II, an ideological statement written in 1973 for the American Humanist Association (AHA). The motto of the AHA is "Good without a God." Denying the existence of "the prayer-hearing God, assumed to love and care for persons, to hear and understand their prayers and to be able to do something about them," the Manifesto stated. "No deity will save us; we must save ourselves." The document is available on the website of the American Humanist Association at https://americanhumanist.org/what-is-humanism/manifesto2/.

promised the suburban housewife that if she'd just get out of the house, find a job she could "take seriously as part of a life plan," and become "economically productive," she would at last become "serene" and "the problem that had no name" would be solved.

By now, of course, we can plainly see this prescription for female happiness hasn't created the glorious utopia on earth Betty promised. It all sounded good on paper to my boomer generation (particularly to those of us entering the workforce), but in real life the theories didn't hold up. Instead, here we are fifty years later, suffering from the aftereffects of an overly sexualized, work-focused form of feminism that's left women treated as sex objects, unborn babies discarded like Dixie cups, and working mothers feeling so stressed and time-pressured that the notion of becoming "completely developed in every way" sounds like a fairy tale.

Why didn't Betty's promises pan out? I hope to answer that question throughout this book. But as a starting point, I'd propose it's partly because Betty got her story wrong on two counts.

First, she oversimplified and *misnamed the problem*. The women she surveyed were no doubt miserable for many reasons, not merely because they were "just housewives."

Second, she oversimplified and *misnamed the solution*. The world of total work has not set women free. On the contrary, "Work will set you free," as history buffs will recall, was the sign the national socialist party in Germany posted over the gates of Auschwitz during World War II—an unholy promise that has never panned out well for anyone.

Greatly influenced by the socialist theories of Karl Marx, which were still fashionable in her day, Betty's real error was materialism. A woman, in fact, is not merely the product of her economic conditions, and it's impossible to make her happy and solve all her interior problems from the outside simply by creating a better economic environment. Betty did not know the lessons Christ taught, one of which is that there's no permanent happiness to be found in the way of the world, the path of personal gain. Following Marx, she implicitly defined the identity of a woman as a "worker" and her life in terms of the "work" she does. Her promise—we as women can create a happy utopia on earth *without God* if only we fulfill and actualize ourselves by earning our own money and working hard in the occupations we choose—hasn't given us freedom. It's given us burnout.

Yet at the same time she misnamed the problem and misnamed the solution, Betty correctly saw that these housewives were desperately seeking *something*. And she further correctly saw that this missing piece in their lives somehow involved their *personhood*. In fact, the quest for *personhood* is what Betty said the women's movement was all about.[26] And this is the central part of the story I'm convinced she got right.

The Quest for Meaning

Certainly, the problem Betty unearthed while researching the *Mystique* was about far more than the deadening boredom of suburbia. It was a summons for us women to reflect more deeply on the meaning of our lives. In our noisy, consumerist society, we as women were so distracted and defined by the images of womanhood presented to us by the media, particularly by the women's magazines for which Betty wrote, we could no longer trust what she called "the authority of the inner voice."

And where did Betty think a woman's authority comes from? Now we come to another Y junction in the railroad tracks where the old 1960s feminism and the new Christian feminism part company.

As the unshakable Alice Paul and other Christian suffragists clearly demonstrated, a woman's true authority comes from her relationship with an infinitely *higher* authority—the authority of the God who created everyone and everything. In John Paul II's words, "The interior life is the spiritual life."[27] We feel incomplete and unfulfilled because we are meant to find our completion—and our fullness of personhood—in self-sacrificial love for God and others. Our deepest strengths lie in our union with God and our defense of truth, not simply in working harder for a bigger paycheck.[‡]

Unfortunately, this higher and deeper dimension of a woman's personhood wasn't on Betty's intellectual radar. She thought her authority came entirely from *herself*. Trapped in an unhappy marriage and soon to get a divorce, she promised women that if they'd just stop thinking so much about others and focus more on actualizing themselves, particularly on earning their own money, building their own careers, and exercising their own talents (a pseudo religion of self-worship that psychologist Paul Vitz has called "selfism"[28]), they'd be free and happy at last. Judaism and Christianity teach we belong to God and by extension others. Selfism (which is perfectly encapsulated in today's "selfie-ism") teaches, "I define myself. I create myself. I belong to me." In a new epilogue for *The*

[‡] Of course, there's nothing *wrong* with a bigger paycheck. Women certainly deserve equal pay for equal work. But when a paycheck or a career becomes an end in itself and the measure of one's worth, it has become a false idol and has replaced God with a transitory goal that can never fully satisfy the human heart.

Feminine Mystique, published in 2001, Betty mused: "What gave us the strength and the nerve to do what we did in the name of American women, of women of the world? It was, of course, because we were doing it for ourselves. It was not charity for poor others."[29]

Yet from a Judeo-Christian perspective, this self-focused, self-sufficient, radically autonomous vision of a woman's personhood leads not to peace, joy, and freedom but to an emptiness Saint Gregory of Nyssa in the fourth century called "the gloom of idolatry"[30] or what Saint Paul called "godly grief" (2 Cor 7:9)—a sad sense that nothing in this world will ever completely satisfy us coupled with a deep human longing for something more. This spiritual longing is one thing that separates humans from the animals. Human persons have this longing. Animals don't. As Saint John Paul II plainly stated, "Nobody speaks convincingly about an animal person."[31] Without a relationship with the God who is self-emptying love, this world closes in on itself and begins to feel like a meaningless prison.

Jewish psychiatrist Viktor Frankl, who witnessed the cruel attempts to dehumanize men and women in the work camps of Auschwitz and Dachau, called this sense of meaninglessness "the abyss experience." What's more, he observed as long ago as 1975 that six in ten of his American students had personally experienced this "existential vacuum."[32] One might expect that in today's increasingly fragmented world—where women and men are continually taught we have to be "independent" of God to be free—those numbers would now be even higher.

In Dr. Frankl's view, this longing for *something more*—this "despair over the apparent meaninglessness of life"—isn't a symptom of neurosis, but rather a human *achievement*.[33] In the Christian understanding of reality, this experience can be God's most precious gift to our souls, because it urges us to open up our hearts and seek him. The Christian woman finds the source of her interior peace—that is to say, her strength and *wholeness* of personhood—in intimate, self-giving *relationships* of love. But, sadly, for many angry, anxious, lonely people in this world today, "the problem that has no name" remains a dark riddle yet to be solved.

Defending the Family

Despite her quest for power and her desire to escape from a disintegrating marriage, it's important to remember that, as the most influential American feminist of the 1960s, Betty never dismissed *motherhood* and *the family* as traps for women (as later, more radical feminists did). Rather, as the mother of three, Betty said motherhood for her had been "delicious."[34] The first edition of *The Feminine Mystique* didn't even mention abortion or contraception.

Even as late as the year 2000, Betty wrote, "Ideologically, I was never for abortion. Motherhood is a value to me, and even today abortion is not.... I believed passionately in 1967, as I do today, that women should have the right of chosen motherhood. For me the matter of choice has never been primarily the choice of abortion, but that you can choose to be a mother. That is as important as any right written into the Constitution."[35]

Nearly thirty years after publishing the *Mystique*, Betty told *Playboy* magazine: "Women are the people who give birth to children, and that is a necessary value in society.... You want a feminism that includes women who have children and want children because that's the majority of women."[36] In answer to feminist Gloria Steinem, who'd called marriage a form of prostitution, Betty retorted, "That extreme form of thinking tends to come from women who hate having to deal with the complexities of juggling a career and a family and so, almost literally, they want to throw the baby out with the bath water. It's just unrealistic to be a feminist who is anti-family."[37]

As she grew older, Gloria (who was famous for saying, "A woman needs a man like a fish needs a bicycle") gave up her scorn for marriage and even got married herself—to South Africa-born British entrepreneur David Bale. Three years after their wedding, Bale died of brain cancer. When asked why she'd changed her views on marriage, Gloria reportedly replied, "I didn't change. Marriage changed. We spent 30 years in the United States changing the marriage laws. If I had married when I was supposed to get married I would have lost my name, my legal residence, my credit rating, many of my civil rights. That's not true anymore. It's possible to make an equal marriage."[38]

Certainly, when it came to the status of women in the 1960s, there *was* much that needed to be changed. Women of my boomer generation were entering the workforce in droves, and we were encountering many unjust surprises. Women were being fired for being pregnant. I can attest to this personally. In 1970, I was fired from my newspaper job for being pregnant (Betty had also been fired from her newspaper job for being pregnant in the 1940s). Classified ads were divided into "Help Wanted Male" (all the good jobs) and "Help Wanted Female" (sales clerks, typists, and cleaning ladies). Women were paid less than men for doing the same jobs. A married woman couldn't apply for credit in her own name. Medical and law schools were often closed to women. Airline flight attendants were fired if they gained weight, got married, or turned age thirty-two or thirty-five.[39] In some states, a woman couldn't serve on a jury. Understandably, working women were quite united in wanting to put a stop to all this. In this mid-twentieth-century milieu (which, you'll notice, sprang more from problems in the *workplace* and *academia* than in the *home*), the feminist push for women to have equal opportunities with men resonated deeply. Such social injustices certainly needed to be addressed—and Betty Friedan seized the reins to address them.

But when Betty took a trip to France and met with existentialist feminist Simone de Beauvoir (philosopher Jean-Paul Sartre's lifelong partner), she was shocked by the French atheist's hostility toward motherhood and the family. Dismayed, Betty wrote:

> The comforts of the family, the decoration of one's own home, fashion, marriage, motherhood—all these things are women's enemy [de Beauvoir] said. It is not even a question of giving women a choice—anything that encourages them to want to be mothers or gives them that choice is wrong. The family must be abolished, she said with absolute authority. *How then will we perpetuate the human race?* [I asked.] There are too many people already, she said. *Am I supposed to take this seriously? It didn't seem to have much to do with the lives of real women, somehow.* Or even with the reality of herself, Simone de Beauvoir, in this salon that was decorated with personal style, full of cherished objects. (Italics added.)[40]

Betty recognized in Simone's totalitarian philosophy what she called "the authoritarian overtones of the supposedly Maoist party line I'd heard before from sophomoric, self-styled radical feminists in America."[41] So once again we see a clear, black line between the moderate mainstream feminism of the 1960s (the kind that attracted me and so many other women of my generation) and the antiman, antifamily extremists who later garnered so much media attention and continue to do so today.

Betty's call for a feminism that included marriage, motherhood, college degrees, and careers contained enough truth that it touched millions of women's minds and hearts in the 1960s. It was the form of feminism that attracted me as a journalist and working mother, and it remains the one form of feminism which, at least on the surface, appears to be compatible with the quest for women's dignity championed by Christian suffragist Alice Paul.

So how did the original feminism I bought into in the 1960s become so corrupt and fall so far from grace? How did we get to the point where feminists are marching in the streets with pink pussyhats on their heads, decrying marriage as a "trap," agitating for the right to be men, and defending the sexual revolution's demand for abortion as the *sine qua non* of women's freedom? How did we get to the point where radical feminists in America today no longer agree with Betty regarding the family but have instead embraced the nihilistic ideas of Simone de Beauvoir and see the family as "a central problem in the advancement of women's equality"?[42]

Sadly, despite all the materialistic career gains upper- and middle-class women have made over the past fifty years, many women still suffer with interior disorder in their lives. Instead of calmness and peace, there's rage and dissatisfaction. Instead of quiet confidence, there's anxiety and fear. Instead of love and joy in community, there is isolation and loneliness. The "problem that has no name" is still with us in search of a solution. Plainly, something in the feminist quest has gone terribly wrong. But what? How and when did it all begin?

In the next chapter, we'll begin to unravel this strange mystery. We'll see when and where the feminist train, in its journey toward greater freedom for women, came to a Y junction and took the wrong track. We'll trace the key events along the way that brought about what might be called feminism's "great derailment." We'll see how what started out in the 1960s as a woman's quest for *wholeness* of personhood led, instead, to a sad *reduction* of our personhood and to a mixed bag of demands many thoughtful people can no longer accept.

2

WOMAN AS A SEXUAL ANIMAL

To understand when, where, and how the feminist train switched to that wrong track and barreled on until it finally went off the rails, we need to look back farther in history to the 1950s. Strange as it may seem, we need to start with the sex research of University of Indiana zoologist Alfred Kinsey. For it was Kinsey's reduction of a woman's human *personhood* to the level of a sexual animal that laid the shaky foundation upon which many marketers began to build and package the notion that a woman's *economic* freedom also somehow requires her to be *sexually* available with no strings attached. This false construct, in turn, has led to massive upheavals in relationships between men and women as well as fear of motherhood, millions of abortions, a multibillion-dollar porn industry, widespread sexual harassment, and a divorce culture so brutal that it's left many young adults terrified to get married.

Without Kinsey's reduction of a woman's personhood to the level of a sexual animal—and without the popular media's unbridled enthusiasm for this idea—our world would likely look very different than it does today. So let's take a closer look at how all this unfolded, so we can more clearly understand and tell others around us how we got from the "Father Knows Best" world of the 1950s to a world where father is presumed to know nothing, especially when it comes to women's issues.

A Long Time Ago

In 1953, Alfred Kinsey published his book *Sexual Behavior in the Human Female* (a follow-up to his 1948 *Sexual Behavior in the Human Male*). This was at a time in America when sexual pleasure and a woman's sexual choices were not considered to be the most important things in her life. Sex was not on every television set, newsstand, and billboard. There was no pornography-littered Internet, and if you had said "same-sex marriage," no one would have known what the heck you were talking about. Marriage was only between a man and a woman, and couples who got married usually stayed married. A child's right to innocence was still cherished and protected. Growing up in the 1950s in a small town in Iowa, I didn't even hear about sex until I was in sixth grade. (Admittedly, I was one of the more innocent ones.)

Further, I knew only one girl in my high-school class whose parents were divorced. Can you imagine? Just one! More hanky-panky was no doubt going on than many people were willing to admit. But, for the most part, Judeo-Christian values toward human sexuality were still assumed in society, and people felt at least some social pressure to resist their animal instincts.

Known as "the father of sexology," Kinsey claimed that modern men and women no longer had to resist their animal instincts, because nobody was following those old-hat biblical "taboos" anyway. What's more, he produced thousands of statistics that supposedly proved his claims. Of the "about 5,300"* white males and 5,940 white females who volunteered to talk about their sex lives and provide data for his reports, 85 percent of the men and 48

---

*Kinsey was no more precise than this.

percent of the women said they'd had premarital sex, and 50 percent of the men and 40 percent of the women had been unfaithful after marriage. Incredibly, 71 percent of these unfaithful wives claimed the affair hadn't hurt their marriages, and a few even claimed their affairs had made their marriages better.

Yet Kinsey was far more than a fact-finder: he was a bisexual social reformer trying to change the sexual mores, attitudes, and laws of a nation. Kinsey viewed a woman's sexual behavior as separate from all her other behaviors, then made what one State University of Iowa sociologist called "a sweeping and indiscriminate plea for [societal] change,"[1] not considering (as all good scientists must) where he might be wrong. Kinsey biographer James H. Jones observed, "Kinsey's views often suffused his prose. Simply put, he could not keep himself out of the text. As a secular evangelist, he had a gospel to proclaim, and he meant to preach it."[2] Pointing to his statistics, Kinsey proclaimed that everything from homosexuality and childhood sexual activity to sex with animals (reportedly experienced by 17 percent of farm boys) was biologically "normal" and hurt no one. Therefore, in his view, science had "proven" at last that Americans should act on their impulses without inhibitions or guilt.

Naturally, the media went bonkers over this red-hot news. Who could dispute such titillating "facts"? Who would even want to try? After all, this was "science"— and, besides, it sold magazines and newspapers lickety-split. Coming out to rave reviews, the 1948 report on men sold an astonishing two hundred thousand copies in two months.

The sexual revolution was first and foremost a media event. Kinsey's name was everywhere, from titles of pop songs ("Ooh, Dr. Kinsey") to the pages of *Time*, *Life*, *Newsweek*, and the *New Yorker*. Kinsey was "presenting facts," *Look* magazine proclaimed: he was "revealing not what should be but what is." Dubbed "Dr. Sex" and applauded for his personal courage, Kinsey was frequently compared to Darwin, Galileo, and Freud.[3] This media avalanche inspired Columbia University cultural critic Lionel Trilling to observe that Kinsey's work had achieved more authority with the public in a matter of weeks than Sigmund Freud had achieved in a lifetime.[4]

The Experts Object

Beyond all this pop-media hullabaloo, however, many astute scientists warned that Kinsey's statistics were seriously flawed and his theory of human sexuality was gravely in need of repair. Kinsey's list of critics—which read "like a Who's Who of American intellectual life"[5]—included anthropologists Margaret Mead and Ruth Benedict; Stanford University psychologist Lewis Terman; theologians Reinhold Niebuhr and Norman Vincent Peale; Karl Menninger (founder of the famed Menninger Institute); psychiatrist Eric Fromm; and more.[6]

Kinsey was perhaps most bitterly attacked for his shabby sampling. He typically presented his statistics as if they applied to "normal," "average" men and women all over America when, in fact, his findings never applied to people in the general population. For the volume on men, Kinsey and his team took sexual histories from about fourteen hundred imprisoned sex offenders, and he admitted including "several hundred" male prostitutes. In the December 11, 1949, *New York Times*, W. Allen Wallis, then chairman of the University of Chicago's committee on statistics, dismissed "the entire method of collecting and presenting statistics which underlie Dr. Kinsey's conclusions." Wallis observed, "There are six major aspects of any statistical research, and Kinsey fails on four."

For his volume on women, Kinsey redefined "married" to include any woman who'd lived with a man for more than a year.[7] This allowed him to include prostitutes in his sample of allegedly "married" women. Kinsey himself confessed his statistics on women were "least likely" to apply to—now listen to this—all Catholic groups, devout Jews, working-class women, women living in rural areas, women over forty, widows, divorcees, and women who had lived for at least a year in the southeastern quarter of the U.S., in the Pacific Northwest, or in the high plains and Rocky Mountain areas.[8] In a review in the *New York Herald Tribune*, British anthropologist Geoffrey Gorer declared "the sampling is so poor that the only reliable figures are those for college graduates in six of the northeastern states."[9] Seeing Kinsey's "facts" for what they truly were (a statistical smokescreen to cover a hidden political agenda), Gorer called much of Kinsey's work propaganda masquerading as science.[10]

As corrupt as Kinsey's science was, the deeper problem with his research—at least when viewed in the context of the feminist quest for *wholeness*—was that he implicitly reduced a woman's *personhood* to that of a mammal (much like a chimpanzee) without free will or an ability to think rationally. A professor of zoology (he was the world's leading expert on the gall wasp), Kinsey repeatedly called women "human animals" and likened the physiology of a woman's orgasm to sneezing. Noting that this ludicrous idea left out all human understanding of a woman, Brooklyn College anthropologist George Simpson declared, "This is truly a monkey-theory of orgasm."[11] He said Kinsey's entire theory of female sexuality was "built on weasel words slipped in to look like close scientific analysis."[12]

Although Kinsey was married to a woman, he was primarily homosexual, and his biographer James Jones wrote, "According to close friends, Kinsey did not particularly like women or feel comfortable in their presence.... Musing on Kinsey's difficulties with women, a friend observed, 'It's something close to disgust with femininity. He doesn't trust it; he doesn't like it.' "[13]

Anthropologist Margaret Mead caustically observed that Kinsey's work suggested no way to choose between having sex with a woman and having sex with a sheep.[14] Since animals are not *persons*, Kinsey made no mention of love or motherhood in his reports. In his 842-page volume on female sexuality, motherhood was not mentioned once.

By separating sex from human relationships, Mead said Kinsey had left young people clueless about sex. Sexual attitudes in America were changing long before Kinsey released his reports. But afterward, those changes rapidly escalated. Complex social changes can never be linked to one or two causes, but the media excitement over Kinsey's false science coupled with the advent of the birth-control pill certainly *correlated* with changes in Americans' sexual attitudes. Between 1958 and 1968, the percentage of Midwestern college women who approved of premarital sex leaped from 17 to 38 percent. By 1975, according to one Gallup poll, 85 percent of college seniors saw "nothing wrong" with sexual intercourse before marriage.[15]

Playboy's Bunny and *Cosmo*'s Pussycat

Kinsey's reduction of a woman's personhood to that of a sexual animal without a mind or a rational soul (that is to say, Kinsey's *misogyny*)[16] entered America through many channels. But one of the first men to turn Kinsey's view of women into a multimillion-dollar empire was *Playboy* magazine founder Hugh Hefner. Kinsey's work was so often praised in the pages of *Playboy* that Hefner became known as "Kinsey's publicist" and even "Kinsey's pamphleteer." In December 1953 (the same year Kinsey's *Sexual Behavior in the Human Female* came out), the first issue of *Playboy* hit the newsstands, featuring Marilyn Monroe on the cover.

Explaining why he chose the *Playboy* bunny as his magazine's logo, Hefner told a reporter that the bunny "has a sexual meaning, because it's a fresh animal, shy, vivacious, jumping—sexy. First it smells you, then it escapes, then it comes back, and you feel like caressing it, playing with it. A girl resembles a bunny. Joyful, joking."[17]

As you'd expect, feminists condemned Hefner's view of a woman as just an animal to be used for a man's sexual pleasure. Reflecting back on Hefner's choice in an interview, Betty Friedan told *Playboy* readers, "The *Playboy* Bunny dehumanized the image of female sexuality. It was part of the feminine mystique. But the image came at us from everywhere—from *Playboy*, from the ads and programs on television. It was the image of a woman solely in terms of her sexual relation to a man, in this case as a man's sex object and server of his physical needs.... That is why it was objectionable. The Bunny may have been cute and fluffy, but it denied the personhood of women.... It denied the whole previous century, when women had fought for rights, including the right to vote."[18]

To expose *Playboy*'s exploitation of women as nothing more than sexual animals, feminist Gloria Steinem went undercover as a Bunny. Her two-part article, which ran in the May and June 1963 issues of *Show* magazine, revealed degrading, humiliating working conditions, heavy-breathing customers, having to undergo a physical that included an internal exam, and "Bunnies" struggling to support children on wages that "averaged far less than the help-wanted ad stated."[19] By reducing a woman merely to a pleasure-giving animal and pretending this image somehow set her "free," *Playboy* certainly deserved to be on the feminist blacklist.

But feminist disapproval didn't stop *Sex and the Single Girl* author Helen Gurley Brown from turning *Cosmopolitan* (put out by the Hearst Corporation) into a hugely profitable *Playboy* clone. Brown's book, a forerunner of *Sex in the City*, came out in 1962 and was turned into a blockbuster movie starring Tony Curtis and Natalie Wood. One grab line on a 1963 vintage paperback cover billed it as the "sensational best seller that torpedoes the myth that a girl must be married to enjoy a satisfying life." In 1965, under the tutelage of her husband, Hollywood producer David Brown, Helen worked to transform *Cosmo* into a female *Playboy*. Pleased with the notion of a female *Playboy*, Hefner helped Helen hire the right people and put her in touch with the same agents and writers *Playboy* was using.

Whereas Hefner chose the bunny as his animal icon for female sexuality, Helen chose the pussycat. In a paradoxical twist that has to go down in history as one of the greatest marketing schemes of the twentieth century, Helen took Kinsey's idea of a woman as a sexual animal and figured out how to sell this image to insecure single women as their path to self-fulfillment and freedom.

In the 1960s and 1970s, Helen was one of the leading women in America promoting Kinsey's reduction of a woman's personhood to the level of a sexual animal. She hadn't trained as a journalist. She'd graduated from Woodbury Business College. But before seizing the editing reins at *Cosmo*, she was one of the sharpest advertising copywriters in the nation. Helen knew how to embed sex-revolution ad copy into everything she wrote, and she taught her secrets to *Cosmo*'s stable of editors and writers.

Although I never wrote for *Playboy*, I did work briefly on staff at *Cosmo* and continued to write freelance articles for the magazine for the next two decades. Although I didn't realize it at the time, as an investigative reporter, I, too, had been sent undercover.

In 1971, the year that I, as an ambitious twenty-five-year-old, landed a job in *Cosmo*'s articles department, not one single woman I knew was hopping into bed with men on the first date, having affairs with married men, or cohabiting with her boyfriend. Not one. If those women were out there somewhere in the world, they were hard to find, and they certainly weren't talking to journalists about their sex lives.

We've already seen that Kinsey's statistics didn't apply to average women. His reduction of a woman's personhood to that of a pleasure-seeking, pleasure-giving sexual animal didn't reflect the way most women were living their real lives. So how were we to find women living this supposedly highly fulfilling, sexually liberated lifestyle and write titillating stories about them when these women didn't actually *exist* in high numbers? As *Cosmo*'s editor-in-chief, Helen had a simple solution: we'd just make them up.

THE RULE OF
HELEN GURLEY BROWN

Whenever a group of people work closely together but differ radically from the society around them, it helps for them to have a "Rule" to guide them as they try to adopt a new way of thinking and embrace a whole new way of life. Following the collapse of the Roman Empire late in the fifth century, for example, Saint Benedict of Nursia retreated from the fractured world and created his famous Rule of precepts for monks living under the authority of an abbot.

Well, as an unholy flip side of that, Helen Gurley Brown had also created her "Rule" for editors and writers like me living under *her* authority. If you didn't follow her Rule, you wouldn't keep a job at *Cosmo* for long, and if you were a freelance writer and didn't follow her Rule, she wouldn't publish your stories. Toe the line or no money for you. It was no accident *Life* magazine called Helen "the Iron Butterfly."[1]

Contrary to popular understanding, a "Rule" is not just a list of rules a person is called to follow. A "Rule"—in the traditional sense that Saint Benedict used it and in the way I'm using it here—is a collection of insights about a way of living, along with practical tips or suggestions ("rules") about how to put those insights into practice. I carefully kept Helen Gurley Brown's Rule in a brown file folder for many years. But I thought I must have accidentally thrown it away because when I was writing *Subverted*, I looked for it maybe twenty or thirty times and couldn't find it. I literally had not seen that telltale list of rules in almost a decade. Then not long ago, I suddenly found it buried in a box of papers in the garage. So I don't have to recall Helen's Rule from memory. I have it on my desk right here in front of me, and I can tell you *exactly* what it said. We used this Rule to change our reader's way of thinking, to dull her conscience, and to teach her how to live in a *Cosmo*-created fantasy world. We taught her how to live a whole new way of life—the *Cosmo* Girl lifestyle. And we did it by telling her intriguing little stories.

The Power of Stories

Stories speak to our hearts. They tell us not only how we *might* live but how we *should* live. That's why we must watch the stories we tell and the stories we trust with a vigilant eye.

As one of the best advertising copywriters in the U.S., Helen Gurley Brown knew how to tell a compelling story, the sort of story with the power to change a woman's mind and heart about her sexuality—and to persuade her to buy whatever *Cosmo*'s advertisers were selling. Jesus spoke in parables (little teaching stories). And so did *Cosmo*. The essential difference between the two was that Jesus's parables reveal truth and *Cosmo*'s stories concealed falsehoods designed to lead our unsuspecting reader into a whole new way of life—and into the snares of our advertisers.

When fabricating stories about "ordinary" women (whom she called "civilians"), Helen writes in her Rule:

"Try to locate some of the buildings, restaurants, night-clubs, parks, streets, as well as entire case histories, in cities other than New York, *even if you deliberately have to 'plant' them elsewhere.* (Italics added.) Most writers live in New York; 92% of our readers do *not.*"

By making up these women and "planting" them in places like Cleveland and Des Moines, of course, we made the sex revolution's then-quite-shocking mores seem far more widespread and accepted than they actually were. "The problem of evil," said fourth-century Church Father John Chrysostom, "is that it is usually disguised as good-ness."[2] Written in the tone of big sister talking to little sister, *Cosmo*'s unspoken message to the young reader was: "Everybody else is doing this—and it's only good, inno-cent fun. So why are you being such a stick-in-the-mud? Relax, and enjoy!"

The seductive marketing story we told at *Cosmo*—sex without commitment is glamorous, "if it feels good, do it"—is still constantly being told and sold to young women today. And if you're feeling lonely, insecure, and afraid not to go along with the crowd, you're more vulnerable to being hoodwinked. It's on those days you're feeling most anxious, depressed, unloved, or ugly that you're most likely to be taken in by the story and most tempted to buy all the stuff the sex profiteers are selling, from expensive perfumes and lacy underwear to antianxiety pills and abortion.

As for finding a scientist who would agree with Kinsey's controversial research, that was no problem for us at *Cosmo*, either. If you couldn't find a real scientist to applaud Kinsey's propaganda or to say something sexually provocative and racy, you could simply make up an expert to quote. One of Helen's rules says: "Unless you are a rec-ognized authority on a subject, profound statements must be attributed to somebody appropriate *(even if the writer has to invent the authority).*" (Italics added.) In other words, it's okay—even encouraged—to invent an authority if you can't find a real expert to say what you want them to say. Then she gives two examples:

Bad: All psychiatrists are basically Freudians.

Better: *According to one practitioner who specializes in group therapy,* "All psychiatrists are Freudians." (Italics added)

Of course, all psychiatrists are *not* Freudians. But now we've invented a group-therapy practitioner to tell us this lie. So, presumably, the insecure reader who longs to be a sophisticated insider will be more inclined to believe it. Did I ever invent an authority? Yes, I'm sorry to report that I did.

In the world according to *Cosmo*, sexual abstinence was not the road to feminine strength but the "enemy of desire," and we warned our reader that if she went "too long" without sex, she could develop sexual dysfunctions. In my article "The New (and Surprising!) Facts about Sex," an imaginary divorcee named "Mary" confesses she's so inhibited after five years without sex that she needs sex therapy to enjoy the new man in her life. Poor sad, inhibited Mary.

Meanwhile, in the world according to *Cosmo*, marriage also kills passion. In my article "When He Doesn't Want Sex," a fantasy woman named Yoko, "a passionate Japanese beauty who works in a Chicago bank," complains, "I've only been able to seduce my husband once in six months, and I'm so angst-ridden I can barely eat. If he doesn't unthaw soon, I'm either going to have to have an affair or sue for divorce."

At *Cosmo*, we also frequently sent the message that getting married can wreck a woman's sex life. Although I myself was happily married, I made up an anecdote about a thrill-seeking magazine editor whom I quote as saying, "I used to be Marty's passionate, wicked mistress. Now I'm just his boring old wife."

I could cite more examples, but you get the drift. The difficulty women had in spotting these lies is that much of the information *Cosmo* published was *true*. *Cosmo* was made up not entirely of lies, but of half-truth, limited truth, and out-of-context truth (which is how French philosopher, sociologist, and theologian Jacques Ellul defined "propaganda"). Surrounding all these little amoral tales about women's sex lives, our reader would find lots of accurate, helpful advice. I wrote one article about "How to Buy a Used Car," for example, and another on "What to Do about Those Horrible, Harrowing Headaches." The difficulty of spotting effective propaganda, wherever you find it, is that it's *mixed up with a lot of truth*. It was primarily the stories we wrote about sex that contained sex-revolution propaganda, and even then many facts and expert quotes in those stories were true.

For example, when I was assigned to write that story on "The New (and Surprising!) Facts about Sex," an editor at *Cosmo* (I never knew who) had managed to track down a *real* gynecologist in Hartford, Connecticut, who agreed with Kinsey's unscientific opinions, and I was told to interview only that particular doctor (who also had a sex-therapy practice) and write a story based on what only *he* had to say. As a dutiful little freelance writer in my twenties who longed to be an insider, I didn't even think to contact another expert who might dispute Kinsey's propaganda. In other words, when it came to ferreting out the whole truth about Kinsey's scientifically questionable "facts," the deck was stacked before the interview even began. In this case, I was a purveyor of Kinsey's propaganda without even knowing what I was doing. I was both the deceived and the deceiver. This was real "fake news" at its most elemental.

How Propaganda Works

The subtitle of my previous book *Subverted* was *How I Helped the Sexual Revolution Hijack the Women's Movement.* So, people often ask me, "How *did* you help the sexual revolution hijack the women's movement?" To understand the answer to this question, you have to understand a bit about how propaganda works. Propaganda is not just a bunch of lies. People frequently think that's what it is, so they think they can easily spot it. "I'm so smart: I can spot a lie when I see one." Propaganda is far more subtle than that. It's part of propaganda's nature—and power—to be concealed and disguised.

So, for example, let's consider how subtle propaganda can be. Edward Bernays, a nephew of Sigmund Freud, pioneered the scientific technique of shaping and manipulating public opinion. In 1928, Bernays wrote a book called *Propaganda*, in which he explained how to *transform the buyer's very world* in order to sell products. So, for example, how do you sell pianos to the middle class? A piano is a high-ticket item. You sell pianos, Bernays explained, by selling the music room.[3] To bring Bernays's propaganda theories forward to the present day, you have all these slick magazines like *House Beautiful* and *Architectural Digest*, in which you show glossy photos of upper-class homes and suggest (without actually saying so) that "all chic, stylish, sophisticated people" have music rooms. Once a woman gets "sold" on the idea that she wants a music room, she'll just naturally think: "Ah! I've got to have a piano!"

Well, how do you sell the latest fashions, pricey makeup, expensive perfumes, hair-styling products, singles travel, contraceptive devices and pills, abortions, and all the other products advertised in a woman's magazine? You sell all those things by selling the "*Cosmo* lifestyle." You make up a lot of little stories about how this is the most wonderful, glamorous lifestyle a woman could ever possibly want—no problems, ladies. Just go for it. This is the way all happy, liberated women are living. Once a young woman buys into the *Cosmo* Girl lifestyle, she'll just naturally think she needs to buy all these other products. We sold ideas and norms about sex that went hand in hand with the hookup model of sexual relationships, and we did it for only one reason: money. We did it to cater to our advertisers.

We were not merely telling titillating little sex stories. No. We were doing far more than that. We were, above all, teaching women and girls *a way of living* that would impel—if not compel—them to buy all the consumer products advertised on *Cosmo*'s glossy pages. I'm not suggesting our editorial content directly made any woman do things she might not otherwise have done. But we did sell particular ideas about casual sex and popularize the story of the single, young, career woman who pursues sex and relationships on her own terms, thus combining feminism with the sexual revolution in an emotionally appealing way.

While writing for *Cosmo*, of course, I took the Pill in my marriage to keep from getting pregnant. Everybody did it (or so I believed). That was simply the way any smart, sophisticated woman was supposed to take charge of her sex life. It never occurred to me that contraception is like a gateway drug to abortion. Once a young woman gets "sold" on the idea that her healthy fertility is a problem (rather like a disease) to be treated and controlled by the medical establishment's concoctions, the idea of having an abortion follows taking the Pill the way the idea of buying a piano follows the desire for a music room.

Erasing Virginity and Motherhood

Implicit in the fictional stories we told was the promise that a woman could be anything she wanted to be— doctor, lawyer, CEO, even a high-priced call girl. There were only two things the *Cosmo* Girl could *not* be if she wanted to be glamorous and cool: she couldn't be a virgin, and she shouldn't be a mother.

It was only after I became serious about my faith and looked back with deep regret on what I had done that I realized the *Cosmo* Girl persona we invented could be and do anything she pleased except for one thing: she could not *in any way* be like the Virgin Mary, Mother of God. Carrie Gress, in her insightful book *The Anti-Mary Exposed*, lays out a strong case for her claim that we're living in an anti-Marian age. She thinks that the anti-Mary movement isn't just a possibility—it's already here. Having worked at *Cosmo* and fully participated in this anti-Mary movement for myself, I'm firmly convinced that she's right.

At *Cosmo*, when I began working there in 1971, we rewrote young women's sexual scripts to erase all signs of virginity and motherhood from the story.[*] Speaking of the lack of children in the magazine as a form of

---

[*] Helen later mellowed a bit on the motherhood theme. But it wasn't until November 1986 that she finally published a special section in the magazine on "Mothers Who Work."

myopia, feminist Gloria Steinem described *Cosmo* as "a fantasy world in which all women look beautiful and have enormous bosoms, and [yet] there's a remarkable absence of children."[4]

Helen Gurley Brown had a favorite needlepoint pillow she kept on a floral love seat in her office; the message stitched onto the pillow read, "Good girls go to heaven. Bad girls go everywhere." And that said it all. At *Cosmo*, we split sex from love (sex is just for fun; if it feels good, do it), we split sex from marriage (it's good to live with your boyfriend), we split women from men (if you don't like him, simply leave or divorce him), and we split sex from babies (take the Pill and if the Pill fails, get an abortion). The unspoken sex-revolution message we constantly sent to our *Cosmo* reader was the exact opposite of the Golden Rule. The most self-destructive unspoken rule in Helen's Rule was this: "If you want to be free and happy, your life shouldn't be about loving God and others. It should be all about loving *yourself.*"

A popular little book in 1971 was titled *How to Be Your Own Best Friend*, by Mildred Newman and Bernard Berkowitz.[5] That summed up *Cosmo*'s reduction of a woman's personhood in a nutshell. The good life was all about *you* defining *you*, that "selfism" discussed earlier in chapter 1. Through the imaginary parables we told, we taught girls that selfishness is a desirable end and a moral good. In answer to the essential existential question "To whom do you belong?" the Christian woman replies, "I belong to the God who created me—and to others." The selfist answers, "I belong only to me. I create myself." It was a surefire prescription for a sad, lonely life.

Whereas Betty Friedan taught that creative work of your own will make you happy and set you free, Helen taught that hard work and *sex without the kids* will make you happy and set you free. That last part was the central message of the sexual revolution. If a young woman wanted to consider herself smart, sophisticated, and cool, she had to be sexually "free" and available, yet at the same time reject having children. This, of course, demands then and now that the two kingpins of the sexual revolution (contraception and abortion) be legal and cheap. When feminist Naomi Wolf, author of *The Beauty Myth* (published in 1990), criticized *Cosmo* for keeping women focused on unrealistic standards of beauty and distracted from deeper issues, Helen snapped back at Wolf during a TV talk-show debate: "There is a conspiracy against women, and I'd be the first to say so.... But getting us to be beautiful ain't the problem! We are encouraged to be mothers, to be pregnant."[6] Helen claimed that what held women back from success in the corporation was the "built-in mechanism in their bodies that allows them to have babies," and she refused to place a child alongside a woman on the magazine's cover.[7]

Unfortunately, a small but articulate group of feminist extremists would later take Helen's attacks on motherhood and carry them even further. In 1983, Jeffner Allen, a feminist philosopher then at the Center for Research on Women at Stanford University, called motherhood "the annihilation of women" and wrote: "I would like to affirm the rejection of motherhood on the grounds that motherhood is dangerous to women.... *A mother is she whose body is used as a resource to reproduce men and the world of men.*"[8] (Italics added.)

"I am endangered by motherhood," Allen continued. Embracing the sexual revolution's "me-first" philosophy perhaps without even realizing she was doing so, Allen concluded that by rejecting motherhood, "I claim *my*

life, body, world, as an end in itself."⁹ (Italics added.) As a
feminist extremist, Allen considered seduction and pregnancy to be "remarkably similar," because "both eroti-
cize women's subordination by acting out and deepening
women's lack of power."[10]

Feminism versus Sex Profiteering

As an antifeminist when it came to sex, Helen Gurley
Brown taught that seduction was not a *denial* but an *asser-
tion* of women's power. If men wanted to use women as
sex objects, Helen saw no problem with that: she was all
for it. She claimed men and women should *both* use each
other's bodies for their own personal pleasure. She urged
the single working woman to let go of her "guilt" and
sleep with any man she pleased, even if he was married—
especially if he was the boss.

   Cosmo taught that the best way to get a man to marry
you (if that's what the self-defined *you* wanted) was to have
sex with him. Then he would presumably fall so madly
in love with you that he wouldn't let you go, and he'd
propose. That was a fiction, of course. In reality, the sexual revolution bred distrust between men and women.
This distrust, in turn, led to more heartbreak, fewer marriages, and more abortions. On the one hand, a single girl
couldn't trust a man to marry her and help her care for
their child if she got pregnant, so she "needed" access to
abortion to protect herself if she became pregnant and the
man walked away. On the other hand, a man who slept
with a sexually "free" woman couldn't trust that her baby
was his, so he was more reluctant to marry her and make
all the financial and emotional sacrifices necessary to love,
raise, and support a child from birth through college.

After *Sex and the Single Girl*, Helen's second book was *Sex and the Office* (1964), in which she continued to teach a woman how to use sex as power to get what she wanted out of a man. In one section of her book on the office, titled "What to Wear to Be Especially Sexy,"[11] Helen offered such big-sisterly advice as this: "If you're small-bosomed, wear a pretty, lacy bra and leave your blouse unbuttoned one button below where it usually is."[12] And, "The contradiction of boy-tailoring on a girl's curvy figure is arousing.... Wear beautifully fitting pants to the office on Saturday overtime assignments. An attractive man I know says he can resist *any* girl in a dress but goes absolutely to pieces when girls wear pants." And this: "When a man is seated at his desk reading a letter, stand just behind him, very close, smelling wonderful, of course, and read along with Mitch—or Mack or Sam. *You'll* finish the letter, but there's no guarantee he can keep his mind on it, especially if you nudge up to him kind of close."[13]

On office affairs, Helen wrote, "No office anywhere on earth is so puritanical, impeccable, elegant, sterile or incorruptible as not to contain the yeast for at least one affair, probably more. You can say it couldn't happen *here*, but just let one yeasty type into the place and first thing you know the bread starts rising!"[14]

Once when asked by a *Wall Street Journal* reporter whether any female *Cosmo* staffers had been sexually harassed in the office, Helen perkily quipped, "I certainly hope so. The problem is that we don't have enough men to go around for harassing."[15] So much for the #MeToo Movement's outrage. An audacious flirt, Helen liked to say outrageous things to get attention. She believed women had the power to stave off most unwanted sexual advances, and if a man sexually came onto a woman at work, he was paying her a compliment.[16]

What Betty Thought about *Cosmo*

So what did Betty Friedan, the mother of the women's movement, think of all this? She called *Cosmo* "quite obscene and quite horrible."[17] Decrying any view of freedom that turns a woman into a sex object as a false freedom that denies a woman's full personhood, Betty said *Cosmo*'s editorial content demonstrated "nothing but contempt for women."[18] Rather than expanding women's opportunities in academia and the workforce, Betty said *Cosmo*'s shallow sex-revolution philosophy reduced women's lives to "an immature teenage-level sexual fantasy," promoting "the idea that woman is nothing but a sex object ... and there is nothing in life but bed, bed, bed."[19] Urging women to boycott products whose advertising was "offensive and/ or insulting to women ... [and] degrading to the image of women," Betty's National Organization for Women (NOW) named *Cosmo* as one of the worst offenders.[20]

In response, Helen told the *New York Times* her magazine was "very pro women's lib," and she wasn't interested in treating women *only* as sex objects, either.[21] Which was true. No matter how often Helen's fantasy "*Cosmo* Girl" might be in bed, she still had to work for a living. The *Cosmo* philosophy was "sex without the kids *and* hard work will set you free."

The feminist quest for economic and academic freedom (as Betty Friedan originally conceived it) and the sexual revolution (as we at *Cosmo* sold it to women) were more than radically *separate* movements. They were dichotomous *opposites*. When she was in the process of founding *Ms.* magazine, feminist Gloria Steinem dismissed *Cosmo* as "the unliberated woman's survival kit."[22] The image of the *Ms.* Woman was designed to be the *Cosmo* Girl's opposite in almost every conceivable way.[23]

So how did these two opposites ever unite to the point that the feminist quest for equal opportunities in academia and the workplace and the sexual revolution's demands for no-strings sexual pleasure now seem to be one and the same? How did we get to the point where so many young women believe that to be "liberated" is to go to college, get a great degree, land a fantastic job, and be as sexually free as possible? At last we've come to the crux of the matter.

The two movements joined forces largely because powerful people in both camps shared one passionate political goal in common: they wanted all abortion laws to be repealed. And here's the big surprise. This unholy marriage might never have been consummated if it hadn't been for Betty Friedan, the woman responsible for inserting the demand to repeal all abortion laws into NOW's political platform.

Hold on a minute. Didn't I say in chapter 1 that Betty was *against* abortion? Yes, indeed, I did. Personally, ideologically—at least for *herself*—that *is* what she said. She'd never had an abortion. She had three children. And she said motherhood for her had been "delicious."[24]

So if she was so against women being treated as sex objects, how did she wind up endorsing abortion and contraception, which hand over women's healthy young bodies to the pharmaceutical and abortion industries, separate sex from babies, and can tempt weaker men and boys just to see women and girls as sex toys? I think it's safe to say Betty didn't *know* the medical dangers of abortion and the Pill. Nor did she know that separating sex from babies can tempt men and boys to turn a woman into a sex object. She didn't know how the masculine mind works. How could she?

Pope Paul VI, however, *did* know how a man's mind works. He knew that anytime you treat sex as an act of *self-taking* instead of an act of *self-giving*, you destroy your own dignity and the dignity of the other person. In his 1968 letter *Humanae Vitae*, the pope warned the world that when you separate sex from procreative love (through the Pill or other artificial methods), many men will wind up seeing women as sex objects to be used merely for their own personal pleasure—the very thing the #MeToo Movement is protesting today with such justifiable outrage. We are all invisibly interconnected in deeper ways than we often realize. This complex, invisible interconnection between sterile sex and the sexual objectification of women completely escaped Betty, as it once escaped me and still escapes most pro-choice feminists today. The sexual revolution was, in fact, a *devolution*, a reverse of evolution, a degradation of woman reduced to the level of a sexual animal but masquerading as progress and freedom.

So Betty's mind fell into a sex-revolution trap. She did a sharp mental U-turn, embraced abortion as a woman's "right," and ruptured the sexual relationship between a man and a woman at its most solid and stabilizing foundation: the creation of a third person. Following in the misguided intellectual footsteps of two men most people have never even heard of (namely, Larry Lader and Dr. Bernard Nathanson), she rhetorically transformed abortion from a violent attack on women (as the suffragists saw it) into an ambitious career woman's "cause." NOW (founded in 1966 with Betty as its first president) embraced the severing of the bond of love between a mother and her unborn child as the *sine qua non* for female freedom. And women around the globe are still bearing the wounds. Not only has China terrorized women with its infamous one-child policy, but as pro-life attorney Helen Alvare succinctly explains, part of the reason many American women still don't have things like flexible workplace hours and maternity leave is because abortion and contraception have "sucked up all the oxygen in the room" when it comes to women's issues.[25]

Let us now go to a moment in American history, a hidden place behind closed doors where abortion was changed, almost in the blink of an eye, from "the ultimate in the exploitation of women" (suffragist Alice Paul's view) into a "reproductive right" women are continually told we must demand and defend if we consider ourselves smart and want to be free.

4

THE MIDNIGHT VOTE IN
THE CHINESE ROOM

The intellectual trap into which Betty fell was set by two upper-class white men who had previously joined forces in the 1960s to repeal all antiabortion laws. One was New York City pro-abortion activist Lawrence (Larry) Lader, a Harvard grad, heir of old money, and magazine writer by profession. The other was New York City obstetrician-gynecologist Bernard Nathanson, M.D., who would one day claim responsibility for seventy-five thousand abortions. Together, these two affluent men co-founded the National Association for the Repeal of Abortion Laws, the forerunner of what is now NARAL Pro-Choice America.

Lader was a sex-revolution extremist, a fervent population controller, and Planned Parenthood founder Margaret Sanger's biographer. A brilliant strategist and master propagandist, Lader said "Maggie" was the greatest influence in his life. Lader understood the interconnectedness of all humanity and had deep insights into how a culture works. He wrote that to tamper with abortion meant the "whole system" of sexual morality in America "could come tumbling down."[1] Which is exactly what happened. To make it happen, he said pro-abortion men had to "recruit the feminists."[2] Because it couldn't be men promoting abortion. That wouldn't be cool. It had to be women. And here's the tipping point: Lader was good friends with Betty Friedan.

Dr. Nathanson, who after seeing a baby on a fetal monitor stopped doing abortions and became a pro-life activist, confessed it was he and Lader (not the feminists) who originally cooked up the idea of "reproductive rights," and they persuaded Betty Friedan to adopt their way of thinking. As you'll recall, Betty was devoted to motherhood and the family, and the first edition of *The Feminine Mystique* didn't even mention contraception or abortion. But Lader was a persuasive fellow. And once he captured Betty's mind and heart, persuading her that women *needed* contraception and abortion to achieve full equality in the workforce and the world, she became an indomitable powerhouse for his cause.

I told the story about Lader and Nathanson persuading Betty to insert the demand for legalized abortion into NOW's political "Bill of Rights" in my book *Subverted*, so there's no need to repeat all the details here. Suffice it to say, the abortion-law-repeal movement, up until the hour feminists took it on, was largely a crusade led by powerful, upper-class, white men, and it was stagnating ... until two of those men persuaded the mother of the 1960s women's movement to do a sharp about-face and join their cause.

I'm often asked: Precisely *how* did those two men convince Betty? What exactly did they *say*? That mystery may never be completely solved this side of the grave. But we do know Lader told Betty that employers didn't want to lose productivity when a mother took time off to care for a newborn or sick child.[3] Lader also wrote a highly persuasive book. Published in 1966, it was titled *Abortion: The First Authoritative and Documented Report on the Laws and Practices Governing Abortion in the U.S. and around the World, and How—for the Sake of Women Everywhere—They Can and Must Be Reformed.* That subtitle plainly revealed the goal of his work. What's more, the book greatly impressed Betty, who gave it a rave blurb on the back cover.[4]

It was Lader, inspired by Margaret Sanger,[5] who disseminated the slogan "No woman can call herself free who does not own and control her own body."* In his book *Ideas Triumphant: Strategies for Social Change and Progress,* Lader bragged he had not only convinced Betty Friedan that women needed abortion to be free (thereby interlocking feminism with his sex-revolution campaign), but he had also gone on to hard-sell his great idea to the U.S. Supreme Court. In the Court's *Roe v. Wade* decision, Lader's *Abortion* book (a masterpiece of propaganda) is cited seven times and the legal papers of NARAL attorney Cyril Chestnut Means (one of Lader's partners in crime) are cited another seven times.[6]

"*Roe v. Wade* was the climactic point in the progress of an idea that had shaken the country as it had rarely been shaken before and had moved from stage to stage in only seven years," Lader gloated.[7] He jubilantly recalled the day after *Roe v. Wade* was announced when leaders of the abortion movement gathered together and celebrated over champagne.[8]

I won't waste your time or mine trying to correct all the errors in Lader's *Abortion* book. It has taken retired

---

*Like most propaganda slogans, this slogan means the *exact opposite* of what it says. In fact, when a girl or woman gets taken in by this slogan and begins to live the hookup lifestyle that will supposedly set her "free," it's usually the business, political, and medical establishments (including the pharmaceutical companies and the abortion industry) who now own and control her body—and are using it as an object for their own profit. Margaret Sanger *did* invent the slogan. But she didn't mean by it what Lader said it meant. Sanger so vehemently opposed abortion that, by Lader's own admission, his abortion advocacy caused a rift between them that remained unhealed at her death.

Villanova University law historian Joseph W. Dellapenna 1,283 pages in *Dispelling the Myths of Abortion History* to sort out all the half-truth, limited truth, and out-of-context truth about abortion that entered into our culture largely through the efforts of Lader and other abortion-advocating male historians. But just to give you a few examples, many statistics in Lader's book—and later in NARAL's press releases—were completely fabricated.

Noting that the first tactic he and Lader used to change abortion law throughout America was to capture the media, Dr. Nathanson confessed, "We persuaded the media that the cause of permissive abortion was a liberal, enlightened, sophisticated one. Knowing that if a true poll were taken we would be soundly defeated, we simply fabricated the results of fictional polls. We announced to the media that we had taken polls and that 60 percent of Americans were in favor of permissive abortion. This is the tactic of the self-fulfilling lie. Few people care to be in the minority."[9] As for the women allegedly dying each year from back-alley abortions, the figure NARAL constantly fed to the media was ten thousand when the real number was around 200 to 250.[10]

The number of illegal abortions done each year in the U.S. was also fabricated. Although the actual figure was about one hundred thousand, Nathanson revealed, "The figure we gave to the media repeatedly was one million."[11] In his *Abortion* book, Lader suggested 1,200,000 was probably the "most accurate figure."[12] According to statistics gathered by Kinsey (whose statistical methods, as we now know, were deeply flawed), only 10 percent of women who aborted their babies suffered any psychological harm—a questionable assumption to say the least.

Impressed by all this, Betty gave Lader's book high praise. So that book seems to have played a role in changing her mind about abortion as a woman's "right." But there's another reason why the abortion "right" might have made sense to Betty. It's the same reason it once made sense to me and other women of my boomer generation. This was a time long ago when women were still being fired for getting pregnant. Corporate America didn't want to hire a woman, train her, put in her in a position of authority, and pay her a high salary, only to have her quit in two years and go home to raise babies. So if you could say, "It's okay, boys. She'll be on the Pill. And if the Pill fails, she'll get an abortion," then equal pay for equal work may suddenly have seemed more palatable to male business leaders—and to Congress.

C. S. Lewis, however, saw the danger of the neutered employee many years ago when he wrote: "As the State grows more like a hive or an ant-hill it needs an increasing number of workers who can be treated as neuters."[13] Further, many women have allowed themselves to be neutered in order to fit into a corporate slot. Helen Gurley Brown was one of them. In her desire for money (she frequently lamented she'd grown up "dirt poor"),[†] she caved in to corporate America's demand for 24/7/365 devotion to the job by becoming a workaholic, taking the Pill, and embracing abortion (when the Pill fails) as her path to success—and through the power of the written word, she enticed other women to follow her lead. With abortion and contraception under her belt, a woman could work "just like a man," win all those juicy promotions, and not have to shortchange the corporation in any way by taking time and attention away from her job to bear children and raise a family.

[†] According to one Helen Gurley Brown biographer, Brooke Hauser, this was largely a fiction Helen made up for "dramatic effect."

Somewhere along the way, "equal" came to mean "interchangeable." Thanks to abortion, the IUD, and the Pill, a docile woman could at last truly become a "female eunuch,"‡ a dehumanized cog reduced to fit into the workforce machine without bother or hassle. In the mid-twentieth-century milieu in which she lived, Betty may have been convinced legal abortion was the only option for some working women if they wanted to stay employed—a diabolic option, to be sure, but a choice that may have seemed practical and politically expedient to her at that time.

For whatever reason, Betty picked up the cry for abortion and the Pill (the two go hand in hand) and rammed what are propagandistically called "reproductive rights" into NOW's "Bill of Rights." Tragically, after Betty accomplished this task, sex-revolution feminists captured media attention, took charge of the public story about what women need to be "free," and have been dominating the feminist conversation ever since.

The Abortion Vote That Changed the World

The abortion vote that changed the world took place on Saturday, November 18, 1967, at NOW's Second Annual Conference, held in the opulent Chinese Room of Washington, D.C.'s Mayflower Hotel. Of just over one thousand NOW members, 105 people (mostly women along with a few men)[14] had gathered to vote on a political "Bill of Rights" that would deeply influence public opinion for the next fifty years and would soon change the laws of a nation.

‡ This was *not* the way feminist Germaine Greer meant the term when she published her international bestseller *The Female Eunuch* in 1970.

A well-connected group of career women in Washington, D.C., had gotten together one day over lunch, and the National Organization for Women (NOW) was born. That night in the Chinese Room, Betty Friedan, as NOW's first president, presided over the meeting.

The NOW delegates voted on eight rights at the meeting. Six of them passed unanimously. One called for a woman's right not to be fired for being pregnant and to have paid maternity leave. A second called for her right to be educated to her full potential. A third for the revision of tax laws to allow working parents to deduct home and child-care expenses.[15] Pretty reasonable stuff.

Only two rights on the table stirred up controversy. One was the call for the Equal Rights Amendment (ERA). After the attendees voted to support the ERA, Black civil rights leader Pauli Murray (the first woman to graduate from Yale Law School and a founder and board member of NOW) angrily stalked out of the meeting and later fired off a letter, resigning from the organization.

When I discovered this in NOW's papers housed in the Arthur and Elizabeth Schlesinger Library on the History of Women in America at the Radcliffe Institute for Advanced Study at Harvard University, I was amazed. I had always just assumed (without evidence) that all fervent feminists had always *supported* the ERA. Not so. Arguing that the Fourteenth Amendment is meant to cover *all* persons, attorney Pauli Murray deeply opposed designating women as a special-interest group separated from the rest of humanity. A devout Christian (she later became an Episcopal priest), she declared that human rights are "indivisible." If our nation's lawmakers had only heard and listened to her feminist voice, we might have avoided the intensely divisive "I-am-my-own-person-and-I-create-myself-and-I-belong-to-*me-alone*" understanding of human rights, which pits the unborn person's right to life against a mother's demand for radical self-sufficiency and underpins the U.S. Supreme Court's holdings in *Roe v. Wade, Doe v. Bolton*, and other controversial decisions.

The second right to create an absolute uproar in the Chinese Room that night was the call to repeal all abortion laws. This isn't the place to retell all that happened there. I previously told that story in my book *Subverted*. But the scene was very dramatic. It was wild. Betty sprang the abortion vote on the delegates as the last issue to be discussed, and the whole meeting spiraled out of control. College students were shouting slogans. One NOW member declared, "I'm against murder." In what sounded like a microcosm of the abortion wars still being fought in our nation today, a huge fight over Right Number 8 raged until almost midnight. And, after the dust settled, the result was that, out of the 105 individuals who originally came to the meeting, only fifty-seven people—*a mere fifty-seven people*—had voted to insert the demand to repeal all abortion laws into NOW's political "Bill of Rights."

Betty said she "felt gooseflesh" when NOW voted to support and fight for the ERA, and she felt "the same thrill" when they voted to include abortion and birth control in their bill of rights. "We were aware that we were making history. And we had an utter confidence that comes from that," Betty wrote. Further, she said that however few women were present, "we understood we had the authority to speak for women over the generations. We weren't thinking about our place in history every minute, and maybe some of us didn't at all, but I certainly had a sense that history was engaged."[16]

After a vote by only fifty-seven people, she believed she'd received the authority to speak for all women over the generations on the subjects of birth control and abortion? Really? It was, of course, the height of hubris. What's more, Betty believed *she* and the fifty-seven in the Chinese Room were "making history," when from a Christian point of view the exact opposite is true. As Martin Luther King Jr. wisely put it: "We are not makers of history. We are made by history."[17] Those who know the Father, the Son, and the Holy Spirit understand *He* is the ultimate mover of history. We're not.

Yet Betty believed she *was* making history—and in a horrifying sort of way she was. For because of the interrelatedness of all things, that small vote she introduced in the Chinese Room has led to a cascade of effects that have brought forth an enormous catastrophe in our nation and the world. At that very hour, shortly before midnight on November 18, 1967, the once-united women's movement split into two factions: feminists *for* abortion and feminists *against* abortion. Truth unites. And what does evil do? It separates and divides. It breaks people apart.

I'm not saying all pro-abortion feminists in the room that night were dupes. I'm saying there was *a split* in the feminist movement at that hour—with some for abortion and others against it. Approximately one-third of the women at that meeting—remember these were all *fervent feminists*—walked out and later resigned from NOW in protest over the abortion vote.

That divisive Plank Number 8 is the only "right" in NOW's political platform we're still fighting over in our nation today. Why? Because that divisive "right" was inserted largely through deception and error due to the influence of two men of whom most people have never even heard: Larry Lader and Dr. Bernard Nathanson.

After the big fight in the Chinese Room, however, all of this was glossed over and NOW's entire Bill of Rights, including the intensely disputed Right Number 8, was sold as a package to the media and the American public.

Betty Friedan was a veteran journalist. She knew how to think with the media, and she knew what the media needed to write an eye-catching headline. In short, she knew how to tell a good story. On Monday morning, after the Saturday-night abortion and birth-control vote, she held a press conference and handed out a press release in which she claimed to be speaking for "28 million American working women, the millions of women emerging from our colleges each year who are intent on full participation in the mainstream of our society, and mothers who are emerging from their homes to go back to school or work."[18]

In short, she grandiosely claimed to be speaking for nearly every working woman and mother in America when, in fact, she was speaking only for herself and fifty-seven people in the Chinese Room. And that's how propaganda works, my friend.

What's more, the media people bought her story. Why wouldn't they? After all, no reporter was allowed in the Chinese Room to witness what actually happened. There's a great difference between an honest reporter being *misinformed* and a reporter consciously making up stories as we did at *Cosmo*. Journalists, after all, are just people. If someone twists the truth, and does it convincingly enough, we're likely to promote lies in our newspapers and magazines, and on Internet sites and the nightly news, without even knowing we're doing it. The media, by its very nature, can offer only snapshots of reality. And masters of propaganda who know how to manipulate those snapshots by telling a good story (using the propaganda tools of half-truth, limited truth, and out-of-context truth to do it) can paint for us a very false picture of the world.

Unfortunately, the public consequences of telling only part of the story can snowball, regardless of the reporter's honest intent. On November 21, 1967, the day after Betty's press conference, the *Washington Post* headlined the abortion vote and reported: "NOW *supports the furthering of the sexual revolution of our century* (italics added) by pressing for widespread sex education and provision of birth control information and contraceptives, and by urging that all laws penalizing abortion be repealed."[19]

Literally overnight, due to the vote of a mere fifty-seven people in the Chinese Room, "reproductive rights" had become synonymous with women's fight for equality in education and the workforce. Although it would take a lot more propaganda to solidify this only partially true story in the minds of the media and the world, the false joining of feminism with the sexual revolution had begun.

5

BEYOND THE CHINESE ROOM

Propaganda (the science and art of molding public opinion) is designed to sell far more than makeup, perfume, and pianos. It's a powerful tool for selling ideas. After a mere fifty-seven people in the Chinese Room voted in November 1967 for legalized abortion as a right that all self-defined "liberated" women desired and needed to be free, abortion rhetoric in America radically—and rapidly—changed.

A smattering of elite groups comprised mostly of upper-middle-class men had been pressing for abortion-law *reform* since the early 1960s. Even before the vote in the Chinese Room, local pro-life movements had been born in some states to fight these men's efforts. But no major organization in America had dared to seek outright *repeal* of all abortion laws—until that small, feisty group of women in the Chinese Room began calling for abortion-law repeal.

Suddenly, in 1968, as U.S. Court of Appeals Judge John T. Noonan observed, "everything changed."[1] That is to say, the abortion story changed. As retired Villanova University law professor Joseph Dellapenna succinctly put it, "Despite the growing mythology that describes the entire birth control movement, as well as the abortion reform movement, throughout the twentieth century as a 'woman's movement,' both movements were largely led by men (especially doctors) until the late 1960s."[2] Not only did the new rhetoric begin focusing on abortion and contraception as consumer products *women* had always wanted and needed to be free, but previous talk of moderate abortion-law reform gave way, seemingly overnight, to bold shouts for radical repeal of all state abortion laws.

One powerful organization to enter the battle for total repeal in 1968 was Planned Parenthood Federation of America. Even after Sanger's death in 1966, her organization continued to oppose abortion. A 1967 report from Planned Parenthood's Eighth International Conference in Santiago, Chile, concluded: "In summing up, it was stressed that abortion is today a widely used method of controlling family size, but it cannot be recommended because of the life and health of the women who undergo it and their future children."[3] In 1968, however, under the presidency of abortionist Dr. Alan Guttmacher, the medical committee of Planned Parenthood-World Federation did a radical about-face in the public square and called for total "abolition of existing statutes and criminal laws regarding abortion."[*]

That same year, 1968, Dr. Guttmacher also changed his rhetoric in a way that dehumanized the baby in the womb. In his 1947 book *Having a Baby*, Guttmacher had referred to fertilization (when the man's sperm fuses with the nucleus of the woman's egg) as a special time: he wrote of "the new baby which is created at this exact moment," and "at the exact moment when a new life is initiated, a great deal is determined which is forever irrevocable—its sex, coloring, body-build, blood group, and in large measure its mental capacity and emotional stability."[4] In 1961,

---

[*] This proposal was approved the following year by Planned Parenthood's broader membership.

Dr. Guttmacher wrote once again of fertilization as that time when "a baby has been conceived."[5]

But in 1968, as president of Planned Parenthood,[†] Dr. Guttmacher suddenly informed the attorneys, law professors, and judges who read the prestigious *Rutgers Law Review*: "My feeling is that the fetus, particularly during its early intrauterine life, is merely a group of specialized cells that do not differ materially from other cells."[6] Due not to any objective new scientific breakthrough but merely to Guttmacher's mercurial new *feeling*, the baby in the womb had been degraded to a *persona non grata*, a nondescript clump of cells called a "fetus," without dignity.

The ACLU Comes Aboard

In its newfound call for total repeal, Planned Parenthood was hardly alone. In late March 1968, the American Civil Liberties Union (ACLU)—a group of attorneys who accepted the rhetoric of the women's movement and nourished a vision of themselves as "champions of the downtrodden" and as "freedom fighters for women"— decided to work for full repeal of all abortion laws "prior to the viability of the fetus."[7] (The "baby" in the womb had disappeared.)

This decision was made despite the objections of some members, including University of Notre Dame law professor Thomas Shaffer, who charged that "the [abortion] reform movement is morally irresponsible because it will not face the possibility that this particular form of birth control is infanticide, that it shatters, therefore, the only certain unity mankind has—its unity against death."[8] In a

---

[†] He became president of the organization in 1962.

letter he wrote to a newspaper, Shaffer protested, "It is not true that abortion is merely an extension of medical science to the pregnant, any more than the careful antiseptic administration of cyanide would merely extend medical science to the aged. The question in either case is whether doctors should be healers or executioners."[9]

Nevertheless, six weeks after the ACLU called for abortion in 1968 without legal limitations, the then male-dominated American College of Obstetricians and Gynecologists endorsed extensive liberalization of abortion laws.[10] Also in 1968, the governing council of the American Public Health Association announced that restrictive abortion laws should be repealed.[11]

Once the controversial abortion vote in the Chinese Room was ratified by all these powerful organizations, the partial story Betty had told the *Washington Post* rapidly became the *only* story the media could hear and report. As Judge Noonan put it, "There was a massive barrier through which any news or opinion contrary to the [abortion] liberty had to travel. There was not a single large urban newspaper regularly carrying the anti-abortion viewpoint the way Horace Greeley's *Tribune* had carried the anti-slavery viewpoint."[12]

This news blackout, in turn, had a predictable effect on American voters. "In the 1976 presidential campaign," a pro-abortion reporter observed, "opinion polls showed a bare 1 percent of the public considered abortion a national election issue."[13]

Through the media's eyes, the American public gradually came to see abortion not as an issue that was *intensely controversial even among feminists* (which was the truth) but as a "civil right" that *all strong, intelligent women* had always wanted if we were ever to be liberated and free. Outside of a tender, mutually loving relationship, of course, sex tends to put one person—usually the woman in relationship to the man—in the position of an object to be used entirely and exclusively for her partner's pleasure. When fifty-seven people in the Chinese Room caved into the sexual revolution's demands, they turned feminism into the playboy's dream come true.

Feminists on the Left Get Angry

Some feminists, ever alert to the sins of the American male but blind to the sins of the American female, found it significant that the vast majority of abortion-law reformers during the 1960s were men. Why? Never one to mince words, radical left-wing feminist Andrea Dworkin declared:

> It was the brake that pregnancy put on [sex] that made abortion a high-priority political issue for men in the 1960s—not only for young men, but also for the older leftist men who were skimming sex off the top of the counterculture and even for more traditional men who dipped into the pool of hippie girls now and then. The decriminalization of abortion—for that was the political goal—was seen as the final fillip: it would make women absolutely accessible, absolutely "free." The sexual revolution, in order to work, required that abortion be available to women on demand. If it were not, [sex] would not be available to men on demand. Getting laid was at stake. Not just getting laid, but getting laid the way great numbers of boys and men had always wanted—lots of girls who wanted it all the time outside marriage, free, giving it away. The male-dominated Left agitated for and fought for and argued for and even organized for and even provided political and economic resources for abortion rights for women. The Left was militant on the issue.[14]

Sexually predatory men quickly picked up on the implications of the so-called new woman's demands for contraception and abortion. That same year of infamy—1968—advertising writer Eric Weber (who described himself as "sexually obsessed") penned his international bestseller *How to Pick Up Girls*. The book, which sold over three million copies and was translated into more than twenty languages, was allegedly credited with kick-starting "the seduction community."[15]

Men who were seeking ways to "love her and leave her" were captivated by such seduction lessons.[16] By the mid- to late 1980s, as *Cosmo*'s casual-sex lifestyle became increasingly the norm for insecure single girls, women's magazines began to be filled with articles about ambivalent men who feared commitment and "Jekyll-and-Hyde" lovers who couldn't make up their minds whether they loved a woman or not. In February 1985, I published a sad but nonetheless true piece in *Connecticut* magazine titled "Ah, Romance ... Where Has It Gone?"[17] documenting the fact that for many couples traditional courtship rules had all but disappeared.

So that's how 1960s feminism—which started out as a noble, *unifying* quest for wholeness of feminine personhood and for economic and educational equity in the workplace and academia—first began to be transformed into a *divisive* sex-revolution vehicle for abortion, contraception, and Kinsey-*Playboy*-*Cosmo*-style sex education, issues that continue to divide strong, liberated women and men to this very day.

Feminists on the Right Walk Out

Hold on here. Didn't I say some pro-life feminists walked *out* of that meeting in the Chinese Room and later resigned from NOW over the abortion vote? What happened to them?

Good question. Let's take a look.

One pro-life Christian feminist in the Chinese Room who *didn't* buy into the illusion that abortion sets a woman free was Ohio attorney Elizabeth ("Betty") Boyer. Fighting against the economic inequalities operating against women at that time, her philosophy was "Give a woman a decent education, a decent paycheck, and don't clobber her with unfair taxes, and she can survive pretty well."[18] She went home in despair over the abortion vote; she knew the women she'd recruited in Ohio would be as appalled as she was. In her words, a new life was "a sacred trust."[19] Boyer later resigned from the NOW board after what she described as "a shouting match."[20] Determined to give women the organization she'd promised them, she went back to Ohio and founded the Women's Equity Action League (WEAL).

WEAL. Ever hear of it? No? Until I started researching all this, I hadn't heard of it, either. When I spoke in Cleveland, even the pro-life leaders in Betty Boyer's own home town hadn't heard of her or her organization. WEAL represented a continuation of what feminism was under the suffragists. This is another forgotten part of history that pro-life feminists may want to reclaim as we speak our minds in the public square.

Although WEAL's membership never exceeded ten thousand, these women did an amazing amount of good work. Betty Boyer and her allies at WEAL worked through litigation and lobbying to—now listen to this list—open up academia to women, force newspapers to stop running "Help Wanted Male" and "Helped Wanted Female" classified ads, and defend a woman's right to serve on a jury. WEAL also worked to get girls' sports programs in high schools, lobbied to get the Pregnancy Discrimination Act of 1978 passed (which made it illegal to fire a woman just because she was pregnant), and was instrumental in the passage of the Equal Credit Opportunity Act of 1974, a law allowing a married woman to apply for credit in her own name.[21]

I'm not saying WEAL won all these victories single-handedly. They worked with other groups on the same issues. For example, Eleanor Smeal (NOW's president from 1977 to 1982) also worked to get the Pregnancy Discrimination Act of 1978 passed. But I do think it's safe to say that the pro-life feminists at WEAL did a huge chunk of the work and pro-abortion feminists received most of the media credit.

To be fair, when I spoke to Betty Boyer's niece, Patricia Bliss-Egan, she said the members of WEAL didn't *want* the publicity. These were professional working women who worried that if their bosses ever found out they were among "*those* women" marching in the streets, they'd be fired.

After winning many legal victories in the courts to create greater equity and dignity for women in academia and the workplace, the leaders of WEAL believed their job was done. They had accomplished many of the goals they set out to achieve. WEAL disbanded in 1989.

And yet, thanks to the deep pockets of pharmaceutical companies, population planners, and other special-interest groups bankrolling their own sex-related agendas, the radical, pro-abortion, antimotherhood, antifamily—and fundamentally *antiwoman*—sex-revolution branch of feminism we promoted at *Cosmo* just keeps rolling on down the tracks. Feminism is now equated not only with abortion, contraception, and sex education in our schools but also with a panoply of other sex-related demands that weren't even on the table in the Chinese Room, including homosexuality, pornography, same-sex marriage, gender ideology, etc. The sexual politics list just goes on and on.

So how did all these other sex-revolution issues get bound up with what's now popularly called "feminism"? When did all *that* begin? Well, that's an interesting story, too. As you'd expect, the ever-present media, who never seem to get things quite right (and often get them quite wrong), played a pivotal role in the story.

6

SEXUAL POLITICS
ENTER THE FRAY

After the debacle in the Chinese Room, Betty Friedan
(who had not been reelected president of NOW and
"wanted an inspiring project to crown her career"[1]) orga-
nized the Women's Strike for Equality. On August 26,
1970, she led a police-estimated crowd of more than
twenty thousand people marching curb to curb down New
York City's Fifth Avenue. Some angry women carried
signs and banners displaying antiman, antihousework slogans like "Don't Cook Dinner—Starve a Rat Tonight!"
and "Don't Iron While the Strike Is Hot."

But as usual, the media reports and photos didn't tell
the whole story. According to Betty's eyewitness account,
perhaps as many as one-third of the people marching in
the parade were *men*.[2] Contrary to popular opinion, the
call for equal economic and academic opportunities for
women in the 1960s and '70s was not a movement exclusively made up of women. NOW was called the National
Organization *for* Women, not the National Organization
of Women. Supportive men and fathers with a strong sense
of justice were also working alongside feminists to help
them achieve their goals. With thousands more marching
in other cities, including Boston, Chicago, San Francisco,
and Washington, D.C., the Women's Strike for Equality

captured huge media attention and established the women's movement for the first time as a powerful political force in the public eye. The strike was successful beyond Betty's wildest dreams. She reportedly called it "the high point of [her] political life."[3]

And precisely at that moment when Betty should have been at the peak of her glory, a thirty-five-year-old upstart—Oxford-educated, Catholic-turned-atheist Kate Millett—swept into the world with her book *Sexual Politics* and stole the media spotlight. Friedan was furious. Featured in broad brush strokes in vivid color on the cover of *Time* magazine, Kate was ordained the "Mao Tse-tung of Women's Liberation," the new "high priestess" of feminism. The article announced: "Until this year, with the publication of a remarkable book called *Sexual Politics*, the movement had no coherent theory to buttress its intuitive passions, no ideologue to provide chapter and verse for its assault on patriarchy."[4] *Sexual Politics* allegedly provided this theory. The man-bashing movement had arrived.

Kate, who oscillated in her life between being a bisexual and a lesbian, had no idea the loudest media voices would anoint her "the Karl Marx of the women's movement." The day after the August 26, 1970, women's march, the *New York Times* listed Kate's name right after Betty Friedan's.

To write *Sexual Politics* (originally her Columbia University doctoral dissertation), Kate searched vigorously through Western literature to find examples of male hatred for women ... and she found them in abundance. Novelists Norman Mailer, Henry Miller, and D. H. Lawrence topped her list of literary abusers. Of all the male literary figures in the twentieth century, Kate singled out French novelist and political activist Jean Genet, a homosexual, as "the only living male writer of first-class literary gifts to have transcended the sexual myths of our era."[5]

Kate adopted a definite position with respect to ultimate things: God was a myth and men were in charge, but they were being brutes. Much as Larry Lader had set himself up as an authority on the history of abortion throughout the centuries, Kate set herself up as an "authority of one" on Judeo-Christian Scripture, sex, and the development of Western civilization, and the media bought into her theories. Recalling the huge media excitement surrounding Kate's ideas in 1970, *New York Times* writer Carol J. Adams (who bought the book when she was nineteen) called *Sexual Politics* "the book that made us feminists."[6] Susan Brownmiller called the excitement surrounding the book "a media avalanche."[7] At one fell swoop, Kate Millett had supplanted Betty Friedan as the media's darling, and Betty's defense of the family (already weakened by her embrace of the abortion "right") now became even more muted in the media world of fantasy.

Calling Simone de Beauvoir her mentor, it was Millett who argued that sex roles are wholly created by culture and that masculinity and femininity are merely "social constructs." It is from her arguments, multiplied thousands of times by later feminists, that we now have all the controversies over men and women demanding to be called by their preferred personal pronouns. Recalling how *Sexual Politics* impacted women of her generation, Adams wrote, "In 1963, Betty Friedan had called the 'feminine mystique' the problem with no name. It was Ms. Millett who gave it a name—sexual politics—and explained the cause: patriarchal society."[8] And with that explosive word—*patriarchy*—feminism and the sexual revolution became so tightly entangled that the media and most Americans could no longer even begin to unsnarl the knot.

The New Enemy: Patriarchy

A sad, tormented figure more to be pitied than emulated, Kate Millett had grown up in St. Paul, Minnesota. Her philandering, alcoholic father left her pious Irish Catholic mother when Kate was fourteen, or at least that's what Kate thought had happened when she was writing *Sexual Politics*. It wasn't until Kate was forty-five years old that her mother revealed *she* was the one who told *him* to leave.[9] But in 1970, in Kate's sexually confused mind, Dad was the enemy who had walked out, leaving her unemployed mother abandoned alone with three children to feed and little means of support.[10]

Kate (who never had children) loved her mother almost to the point of idol worship. As eighty-eight-year-old Helen was slowly dying from a brain tumor, Kate penned a 308-page eulogy to her mother titled *Mother Millett* in which she wrote: "It is a long time since Helen Feely Millett has been as we once knew her.... In a sense we lost her even before we lose her now, the going from us gradual, as if we were being seasoned to bear it finally. Only by degrees having to take on that dreadful singular state in the world—motherlessness."[11]

Yet as much as she loved women, Kate despised men and projected her hatred onto God the Father. As strange as it may sound, a careful reading of her book suggests she seemed to think God was competing with her for power. Her veiled, largely unspoken philosophy seemed to be: saying *no* to God means saying *yes* to me. In *Sexual Politics*, she sweepingly dismissed God as a mere fantasy figure invented by men to dominate women. "What lingers of supernatural authority, the Deity, 'His' ministry, together with the ethics and values, the philosophy and art of our culture—its very civilization," Kate wrote, "is of male manufacture."[12]

To construct her ideas on reordering power in male-female relationships, Kate said she was "deeply indebted" to University of Bristol political-science scholar Ronald V. Sampson and his book *The Psychology of Power*. The Triune God (one God in three Persons) has revealed himself to be all-powerful *and* all-loving, the source of all peace and joy. But Sampson (and Kate by extension) saw love and power as complete opposites. "To pursue the path of virtue and emulate the good is not only not the surest way to rise in the world. It is incompatible with so doing, for goodness and power are antithetical," Sampson declared. "Goodness does not consist only of powerlessness, but where love is, power is absent."[13] He then went on to quote rationalist philosopher Bertrand Russell:

> "Love thy neighbor as thyself" is a positive precept. But in all Christian communities the man who obeys this precept is persecuted, suffering at least poverty, usually imprisonment, and sometimes death. The world is full of injustice, and those who profit by injustice are in a position to administer rewards and punishments. The rewards go to those who invent ingenious justifications for inequality, the punishments to those who try to remedy it. I do not know of any country where a man who has a genuine love for his neighbor can long avoid [being vilified].[14]

Sampson added that it had been the central contention of his own book that Machiavelli was right to insist that practicing power politics couldn't by any logic be reconciled with the precepts of Christian morality.[15] In other words, a love of political power will always vilify and condemn the power of God's love. A point well taken.

So what was Kate's solution to all this if women wanted to be powerful and "free"? Her solution was to restructure all of Western civilization by doing away with the family and getting rid of Christianity, which she rancorously dismissed as "the religion of the inferiority complex (humility)."[16] She failed to understand that true humility, as C. S. Lewis wrote, "is not thinking less of yourself; it is thinking of yourself less." Sadly, Kate's love of political power led her to condemn the power of God's love, just as Sampson said it would.

Much as Lader had done when he penned his book on abortion, Kate set herself up as an "authority of one" on the Bible, Christianity, and the history of Western civilization—and the media world bought into her theories. There's much to deconstruct in Kate's construction of patriarchy (far more than I have the time or inclination to go into here). I would urge any Christian feminist who feels called to tackle this much-needed challenge to begin by reading *Sexual Politics* and also by checking out chapter 4 in *The Subversion of Christianity* by Jacques Ellul. For my part, I think it's enough to say here that in her intellectual self-sufficiency (that is to say, in her self-absorbed intellectual pride) Kate made many historic, anthropological, and sociological errors. But her fundamental error was theological.

Struggling with a seriously unbalanced view not only of sexuality, history, and virtue but also of Scripture, Christ, and the Catholic Church, Kate got hung up on what she called one of "the leading myths of Western culture"—the Fall—which she blamed entirely on Eve, overlooking Adam's complicity in the matter. Never mind the female saints. Pay no attention to Mary Magdalene, apostle to the apostles. Forget about the Virgin Mary, Mother of God—the New Eve, who gave birth to Christ through whom all repentant sinners are forgiven and granted the gift of eternal life. Ignore the many strong, dedicated Christian women down through the centuries who fought, and sometimes died, as martyrs to defend the integrity of the Faith and with God's grace helped to build Western civilization. In Kate's mind, Christianity was all about male dominance.

It is clear that the imaginary God whom poor Kate made up in her mind was exactly opposite to the real Christ. As Caryll Houselander wisely put it in *The Reed of God*, "Our conception of Christ colors our whole life; it informs everything that we touch with its spirit; it makes us what we are." To the degree that we have a false conception of God, which we confuse with the real God of Revelation, Houselander continues, "we restrict and narrow our interests and sympathies; we grow in intolerance and hardness or in a flabbiness which turns to a rot of sweetness like a diabetes of the soul."[17] In Kate's mind and heart, Christianity and Western culture were all about men, particularly male dominance and power. She bitterly sniped, "Patriarchy has God on its side."[18]

Unfortunately, the patriarchy and the matriarchy, at least as Kate imagined them, were false intellectual constructs from the get-go. To split men and women apart and to think you have somehow seen a new reality is a form of foolishness born of intellectual pride. God made all creation new not through men standing independently alone nor through women standing independently alone but through Jesus Christ (both God and man) born from his virgin mother Mary (a woman). That is to say, God made all creation new through the God-baby conceived in the womb of a human woman. And they lived on earth as mother and Child eternally joined *together* in a perfect union of self-giving love.

Although it's certainly true that women down through history frequently haven't received sufficient public credit and respect for all their hard work, it's equally true that strong men and strong women built Western civilization by working *together*. To split men from women—or to pit men *against* women, fathers *against* mothers, and mothers *against* babies—and then somehow imagine you've created a profound new paradigm worthy of emulation is to submit to illusion.

Sadly, since Kate first penned her diatribe against God the Father and men in general, many radical feminists have followed in her footsteps. They seem to consider male faults to be the source of all evil in Western civilization—and Christianity gravely in need of reform—simply because so many people who call themselves Christians aren't exactly models of virtue. But as Frank Sheed wrote decades ago in *Theology for Beginners*, "It is by the saints, and not by the mediocre, still less by the great sinners, that the Church is to be judged. It may seem a loading of the dice to demand that any institution be judged solely by its best members, but in this instance it is not. A medicine must be judged not by those who buy it but by those who actually take it. A Church must be judged by those who hear and obey, not by those who half-hear and disobey when obedience is difficult."[19] Unfortunately, Kate and those women who embraced her divisive way of thinking didn't seem to understand this distinction.

Family Feminism versus Sexual Politics

So, what did Betty Friedan, the mother of second-wave feminism, think about Kate Millett's views of human sexuality as the primary feminist battleground? When asked in 1970 what she thought of "the new trend in the women's movement which seems to be primarily concerned with orgasm, sexual relationships, etc.," Betty told *Social*

Policy magazine, "I'm quite disturbed by it. I think the whole trend is highly diversionary. It builds up a straw-man enemy by packaging together all the negative characteristics in man and making him the main enemy, the oppressor." Betty said that "if the main enemy is seen as the man, women will wallow around in self-pity and man-hatred and never really be moved to action."[20]

Millett's angry attack on men, multiplied thousands of times by those feminists who followed in her footsteps, has split women from men in ways that have broken up loving relationships and damaged us all.

Once again, just as it had happened that night in the Chinese Room, the feminist movement was split by faction into two competing camps. On one side, Kate Millett said: "Sex is deep at the heart of our troubles."[21] On the other side, Betty Friedan said: "The sexual relationship is not the issue."[22] Kate attacked men, hated the family, and spoke of "sex" as an entity that stood alone, isolated from love (the way Kinsey, *Playboy*, and *Cosmo* saw it). Betty defended men and the family and spoke of the sexual *relationship*. She predicted sexual politics would lead the upcoming generation to "turn their backs completely on love and sex and marriage and having children," and, further, she stated in 1970 that this was already happening.[23]

Betty added,

> Unfortunately, the new sexual theorists do not seem to see the possibility of sex and love combined, of joyful sex as part of a larger, meaningful relationship. And some are badly exaggerating the presumed positives of lesbian sex. We don't want a society in which there are two separate sexes, men and women, with each getting their pleasure by themselves—men with men and women with women. Such a vision is hardly the radical future.

It is only pseudo-radical because it does not lead to any real institutional change of any kind. In essence, we cannot permit the image of women to be developed by the homosexual. The male homosexual omits the strength of women just as the bull dyke omits the essential tenderness of men. What is the point of reacting against one's sexual role as a man or woman merely to adopt the stereotype of the opposite sex?[24]

Oh, my goodness! What would she say today? And, remember, this is the *mother of modern feminism* talking. Betty further stated that women need allies and men are important allies. But sexual politics bitterly divides men and women. Unfortunately, as "women were the scapegoats before," Betty declared, "so now man is becoming the new scapegoat, the monster."[25]

As a primary mouthpiece for the sexual revolution, *Cosmo* didn't see man as the monster. *Cosmo* saw the baby in the womb as the monster. Prevent the baby (through contraception) or liquidate the baby (through abortion), and everything would be fine. The sexual revolution was "good." All chosen sexual pleasure in any form was "good." Men were "good." The baby who appeared as a copulatory surprise was "bad." The baby in the womb was *Cosmo*'s scapegoat.

But that was the sex-revolution worldview we promoted at *Cosmo*. With sexual politics, feminism went off on a radically different tangent. What's more, as an inside eyewitness, Betty Friedan saw what was happening. Fighting against the media world of fantasy as vigorously as she fought for justice for women and families, Betty later recalled that the man-haters were given publicity far out of proportion to their numbers in the movement because of the media's hunger for sensationalism. With this I certainly agree.

Whereas Betty defended the family, Kate attacked it. Having grown up with an alcoholic dad and seeming to have no Christian concept of the father as a beloved, loving *servant* to his family, Kate quoted nineteenth-century legal historian Sir Henry Maine, who wrote of *pre-Christian* times: "The eldest male parent is absolutely supreme in his household. His dominion extends to life and death and is unqualified over his children and their houses as over his slaves."[26] From such evidence she went on to make the sweeping claim, "Patriarchy's chief institution is the family,"[27] and then to conclude that if women were to be freed from their sexual "oppression", this "patriarchal family" must be destroyed.

And where were we to find a role model for this destruction of the family? In Kate's view, the Soviet Union had at least some of the answers. She wrote:

The Soviet Union did make a conscious effort to terminate patriarchy and restructure its most basic institution— the family. After the revolution every possible law was passed to free individuals from the claims of the family: free marriage and divorce, contraception, and abortion on demand. Most material of all, the women and children were to be liberated from the controlling economic power of the husband. Under the collective system, the family began to disintegrate along the very lines upon which it had been built. Patriarchy began, as it were, to reverse its own processes, while society returned to the democratic work community which socialist authorities describe as matriarchy.[28]

Kate recognized and regretted the fact that "the Soviet experiment failed and was abandoned."[29] She wrote: "Twenty-seven years after the revolution, the Soviet position had completely reversed itself. The initial radical freedoms in marriage, divorce, abortion, child care, and the family were largely abridged and the reaction gained so that, by 1943, even coeducation was abolished in the Soviet Union. The sexual revolution was over, the counterrevolution triumphant."[30]

Of course, 1943 was in the middle of World War II when Russia had already lost millions of men. That in itself would have necessitated the restructuring of society because many of the men weren't around. They were dead.

In any case, Kate blamed what she called this return to "patriarchy" largely on the inadequacies of Marxist theory, which "had failed to supply a sufficient ideological base for a sexual revolution."[31] She specifically blamed philosopher Friedrich Engels, who "had supplied nothing but a history and economy of the patriarchal family, neglecting to investigate the mental habits it inculcates."[32] She added, "Therefore, with the collapse of the old patriarchal order, there was no positive and coherent theory to greet the inevitable confusion."[33] Kate's ambition was to provide that coherent feminist theory of power—and sexual politics was her answer.

What's more, at age thirty-five, Kate saw something forty-nine-year-old Betty seemingly failed to see and what I failed to see for many years: no-fault divorce, unmarried sex, contraception, and abortion on demand were—and are—direct attacks on the family.

So now at last we can see how and where Betty's original call for a family feminism (which included men and children) began to be silenced in the public square. The subversion began when Betty unintentionally undermined the family by ramming through the demands for legalized abortion into NOW's "Bill of Rights." But the subversion picked up steam when *Sexual Politics* burst onto the scene. Kate Millett became the media's new high priestess of feminism. Her antifamily theory of "patriarchy" as the enemy flooded into the culture. And amid the media's excited shouts for sex without children, Betty's family feminist voice was muted. Soon it became nearly impossible for the American public to tell feminism and the sexual revolution apart. What began as a quest for wholeness of personhood had morphed into a quest for sex, money, pleasure, and power. The once radically separate movements had become one and the same in the eyes of the media and the world.

So whatever happened to the *wholeness of personhood* Betty Friedan originally said the women's movement was all about? Whatever happened to the quest to solve "the problem that had no name"? Amid all the media excitement over sexual liberation, the interior quest that started it all seemed to have been forgotten. Sex-revolution feminists paid lip service to the notion that if women would just follow their lead, everyone would be happy. But, sadly, even Helen Gurley Brown and Kate Millett found no peace in the counterfeit, sexualized, pseudo-feminist philosophies they'd constructed and sold to the world.

At age seventy-two, in an interview with *Psychology Today*, Helen admitted that despite all her success, fame, and fortune, she was miserable and didn't know why. "Isn't it a shame that I can't just be thrilled and happy that I have had this wonderful magazine and a terrific husband?" she confessed to *Psychology Today*. "We're both healthy; we've done okay financially. [She and David were married over fifty years, and they were multimillionaires.] Why can't I be happy about that? I really can't." Sadly, the woman who bragged all her life of "having it all" (except children) admitted it was no fun to wake up "scared every morning."[34]

Tragically, as Helen's own life revealed, when we passionately work ourselves into an exhausted frenzy until we at last acquire all the sex, power, status, money, pleasure, and other self-gratifying idols we crave—when we finally "have it all"—we discover to our great despair that all this stuff was not what we truly wanted, after all. Only after we've grasped the coveted brass ring do we find out it was a worthless illusion that slips through our fingers like sand. What fourth-century saint Gregory of Nyssa called "the gloom of idolatry"[35] still haunts many women today. As an anonymous twentieth-century Carthusian monk simply put it, "We think too much about our own wretched selves, and that is why we are so unhappy."[36]

"This 'self' as we call it ... is not our true and whole being; it is only a part, and the tiniest and least interesting part," continues our anonymous monk. This "false and inferior self" is made up of traits like our age, how fat or thin we are, our health, our successes and failures, what others think of us, and other transitory things—all mere wisps in the wind if they're not viewed as part of the plan of Divine Love.[37] The false "self" that seeks to live for itself alone, wrote twentieth-century Trappist monk Thomas Merton, "is pure illusion." Ultimately, anyone who lives for and by this illusion "must end either in disgust or in madness."[38]

In poor Kate Millett's case, it was the latter. Childless and committed to mental-health institutions off-and-on during her life, she divorced her husband of twenty years, and following a series of lesbian affairs, eventually married her lover Sophie. In a 1998 piece she penned for the *Guardian*, headlined "The Feminist Time Forgot," Kate confessed at age sixty-three: "I have no saleable skill, for all my supposed accomplishments. I am unemployable. Frightening, this future. What poverty ahead, what mortification, what distant bag-lady horrors, when my savings are gone?"[39]

This was a woman who at age thirty-five had her face on the cover of *Time* magazine, then the most influential periodical in the nation. Author of a flaming bestseller, she'd been proclaimed around the world to be the "high priestess" of feminism, one of the most influential social movements in American history. Freed from all conventions, she had "defined herself" and her sexuality entirely in her own way. Yet here she was forlornly complaining of "a life without purpose," "loneliness," and a "sense of failure." She wrote of other feminists she knew who had "vanished into asylums" and of three who "chose" suicide rather than face one more day of meaninglessness.[40] Kate died on September 6, 2017, in Paris at the age of eighty-two. Yet, during the previous fifty-eight years of her life, she had attempted suicide six times.[41]

Unfortunately, the chain of events we've followed—from Kinsey's reduction of a woman to a sexual animal to Kate Millet's view of sex as power—has infiltrated and infected our entire media world. Betty Friedan had said that any view of "freedom" that turns a woman into a sex object is a false freedom that denies a woman's full personhood and shows "nothing but contempt for women." And yet this misunderstanding of what it means to be a free woman has polluted the very air we breathe. It's there in the *New York Times*, the *Washington Post*, on the nightly news, on the Internet ... everywhere. It's especially there in what's left of the women's magazines.

That's not to say pro-life Christians should hate the politically liberal media. Christ never told us whom we should hate. He only told us whom we should love: He said we should love *everyone*. But neither does this mean we should roll over and passively allow the media's intellectual errors to swirl around us without asking questions and without correcting our media friends in love when they provide inadequate answers. When a friend makes a mistake, the friend is still a friend, but the mistake is still a mistake—and we are obligated to point out those mistakes in a spirit of true friendship.

That said, by following the Kinsey-*Playboy*-*Cosmo*-*Sexual Politics* reduction of a woman's personhood to its bitter end, we have come to a place of dense darkness. Women are being sexually harassed at work. Worldwide pornography (sex without love) is a nearly $100-billion-a-year industry, and children are exposed for the first time to porn at an average age of eleven. Half of all marriages end in divorce, sexual abuse is rampant, and fatherless homes in some communities have become the "new normal." Among African American babies who survive long enough to reach the maternity ward, seven in ten are born to single mothers.[42]

All around us in Hollywood, in books, in women's fashion magazines, on television, radio, and the Internet—literally in the air waves we breathe—Kinsey's ugly, reduced, sexualized view of a woman's personhood is on display in gaudy bright lights. And our children and teenagers are being sexually abused and perverted—even in places and by people once thought to be sacrosanct. The whole world is bound up in this chain of darkness.

"Life is not about God and others!" advertisers and *their* media (not ours) scream at us 24/7/365. "Life is all about YOU and YOUR needs! God (if there is a God or gods) is far away in a place called 'heaven,' and you're here on earth to define YOURSELF as YOUR own god in YOUR own way. So be 'empowered' and 'happy' and sexually unrestrained: work hard so you can afford to buy all this stuff we're selling, and set yourself freeeeeeee." This media-fueled, self-gratifying, consumerist fantasy train pretends to be the vehicle conveying women and all of mankind on a liberating fast track leading to a self-defined nirvana filled with unimaginable power and delectable pleasures. Yet at the end of the day, when the train of endless self-gratification at last pulls into the station, its final destination is only fear, loneliness, emptiness, and death.

7

A NEW HOPE RISES

Most women's magazines today are hard-selling *Cosmo*'s highly profitable, self-centered, sexualized feminist mind-set to women, and they've been doing it for decades. As we've seen, legalized abortion on demand (when contraception fails) is only one part of this mindset, but it's an essential component. In 1986, when legal abortion was heavily under attack and I was still freelancing for *Cosmo*, Helen Gurley Brown sent out a slew of invitations to women's magazine editors in New York City, inviting them to have lunch with her and Kate Michelman, then the executive director of the National Abortion Rights Action League (now NARAL Pro-Choice America). As you'll recall from chapter 4, this is the organization Larry Lader and Dr. Bernard Nathanson founded in order to get all abortion laws repealed. In response to Helen's invitation, editors came to the meeting from *Good Housekeeping*, *Redbook*, *Harper's*, *Elle*, *Savvy*, *Family Circle*, *Ladies' Home Journal*, *Glamour*, *Self*, *Parents*, and the now-defunct *New Woman* (where I was a contributing editor). *Ms.* and *Mademoiselle* also sent representatives.[1]

Helen spoke at the meeting, and the editors agreed to run pro-abortion articles in their March 1987 issues. Among the articles that appeared in *Cosmopolitan* that month were "Abortion: Your Right Under Attack,"

"Choice: Separating Myth from Fact," "My Illegal Abortion," and an article on why eight famous women were pro-choice.[2] (One technique of effective propaganda is to find famous "opinion leaders" to promote your cause.)

So let's plainly state what happened here. Editors from more than a dozen powerful women's magazines—a literal army of opinion-makers—got together for lunch one day in New York City and colluded to solicit and publish articles designed to hard-sell *Cosmo*'s politically liberal, pro-abortion, sex-revolution-linked version of feminism to American women.

Was this a form of free speech in action, an example of independent journalists honestly struggling to serve women's best interests and the public's right to know? No. It was a deliberate attempt by a handful of elite women to shape political policy in our democracy—not through a free, open, and unbiased dialogue and exchange of ideas, but through what amounted to a carefully crafted propaganda campaign.

That was in 1987, and the pro-choice feminist movement promoted by the women's media didn't stop there. In 2003, Myrna Blyth (*Ladies' Home Journal*'s editor-in-chief from 1981 to 2002) exposed in more detail how the women's media world works. In *Spin Sisters: How the Women of the Media Sell Unhappiness—and Liberalism—to the Women of America*, she unveiled the mindset of those "members of the female elite media, a Girls' Club of editors, producers, print and television journalists with similar attitudes and opinions who influence the way millions of American women think and feel about their lives, their world, and themselves."[3]

One of the central tenets of sexualized feminism—abortion—was, in Blyth's view, "*the* binding pledge" of the Spin Sisters' sorority, the singular issue "on which there can never be any equivocation or discussion. Listening to them chatter at an editorial meeting or over cocktails, one learns that, according to these experienced politicians, abortion is unquestionably the most important issue for all women in America.... To keep the support of the Spin Sisters, politicians may not stray even a hair from the Planned Parenthood position, and probably neither can the writer in the cubicle next door."[4] As one of those writers (not in a cubicle but freelancing from home), I know from personal experience she was right. What's more, these powerful media women seem to believe that they—and they alone—speak for all smart women and thinking feminists in America and around the world.

If this were the end of the story, it would indeed be a sad, hopeless tale. Is the story over? Have the rich, powerful superachievers won? Happily, no. One of the central strengths of our democracy in the U.S. is that we're a large nation made up of diverse people with widely different (often clashing) opinions. Propaganda put out by organizations like NARAL and Planned Parenthood works very effectively on female magazine writers and editors in New York City (as it once worked well on me). But it doesn't work nearly as well in cities like Cleveland, Omaha, and Salt Lake City, or in small towns in Texas, Kansas, and Arizona.

Sex-revolution feminism has seized the pinnacles of media power in this nation. There's no doubt about that. Sex sells. But on a grassroots level (where power really resides), millions of well-organized, interconnected, pro-life Christian feminists are still fighting for genuine respect and dignity for the authentic personhood of all women—young *and* old, healthy *and* unhealthy, rich *and* poor, born *and* unborn. They're well-organized in a vast, interconnected army of love, and they're encircling others everywhere with their peace, joy, and hope.

An Unknown Soldier

My dear friend and godmother Margot Sheahan, who died in 2005, was one of them. Margot experienced the painful heartbreak of the sexualized feminism's false promises in an intensely personal way: as a mother. One week after graduating from high school, her eighteen-year-old "liberated" daughter ran away with her boyfriend, only to appear six weeks later on their doorstep, tearful and pregnant. As president of Arizona Right to Life, Margot was mortified. Naturally, the baby's father (who'd sworn his undying love for the girl) immediately abandoned her and moved out of state. "May God forgive me," Margot confessed; "my first thought was abortion." But that thought was fleeting. For Margot had deep faith. She knew that through the Cross, joy has come into all the world. She knew how to find the meaning of life and surprising joy through suffering love.

So she embraced the joy of a newborn child. Instead of succumbing to fear, anchored in the strong convictions of their faith, Margot and her husband, Bob, became like unshakable pillars to which a scared, little pregnant mother could fasten herself and attain a firm footing. Unable to do anything to ease their daughter's painful feelings of abandonment and loneliness during her pregnancy, time and again Margot gently reminded herself, "Let go and let God."[5]

When their grandson was born, Margot recalled, "We loved little Joseph from the very first moment we saw him. We loved his oversized hands and feet, how he gazed up at us with his huge dark eyes. He was perfect. He was part of us. Joseph belonged in our family. We loved him unconditionally."[6]

And yet ... just when they thought they were done with raising children, she and Bob sacrificed their new-found freedom to help care for a baby. "We found our-selves bouncing a Rock-a-Roo with one foot, while Joseph waited for a bottle. The baby swing cranked back and forth while we tried to watch TV. The washing machine swished constantly. Baby bottles, receiving blan-kets, diapers and toys lay about. We had to adjust all over again to the clutter and noise that accompany a baby in the home."[7]

Faced with the hard realities of life, Margot didn't take the easy, "it's-all-about-me" way out of a difficult situation. Rather, in her devotion to Christ, she chose the harder and more meaningful path of radical self-giving love. By taking responsibility for the needs of others, she expressed her full *personhood*. And she didn't stop there. After help-ing her own daughter and grandson, Margot then went on to found a twelve-step program called Unwed Parents Anonymous (later The Whole Parent) to help other single mothers and fathers handle the frustrations, loneliness, and other trials that inevitably crop up when one chooses the difficult path of love and struggles to raise a child alone. As a mother to all, when her protégés were ready, Margot also taught young men and women who came to her meet-ings how to abstain from casual sex until they could find authentic pathways to romance, marriage, and true hap-piness. Motherliness has no limits when it comes to love.

Margot regarded abortion as "the great unspoken pain that hangs over our [Unwed Parents Anonymous] meet-ings; though seldom mentioned, it is always there. When the subject is raised the women's voices rise in abortion's painful defense stating, *'I had to do it!'* or *'I didn't know!'*

The men say nothing but simply fold their arms and clench their jaws. Abortion sends us into a dark alley with an impenetrable brick wall of pain at its end."[8]

Margot was never famous. She was never a well-heeled, high-wattage superachiever like those New York City magazine editors sketching out their propaganda campaigns while sipping cocktails and dining on caviar. At the end of her life she was wheelchair-bound, taking dozens of prescription drugs, and in chronic pain. In many ways, she lived and died as anonymously as the program she founded. Yet through grace, in her radical, self-emptying love for God and others, her actions personally transfigured a painful tragedy in her daughter's life into the joyful gift of new life.

A Humble Example

"The Gospel is more than a lesson, much more; it is an example," wrote French priest Raoul Plus.[9] In order to make a doctrine dynamic, we must seek to embody it, to make it incarnate, to give it a body. Through Margot's example, I learned the truth that every woman deserves to be respected not for what she *does* but simply for who she *is*. In the old pro-choice feminist view, we women were valued for how we look and the sort of work we *do*. Full-time mothers were looked down upon as "less important" than high-wattage career women. In the new pro-life feminist vision, all women—including mothers—are valued simply for who they *are*.

When on the evening of October 26, 1985, Mother Teresa of Calcutta—clad in sandals and a blue-trimmed sari—addressed the General Assembly of the United Nations in New York City, U.N. General Secretary Javier Pérez de

Cuéllar introduced her as "the most powerful woman in the world"[10]—a point well taken. Then seventy-five years old, she had won the 1979 Nobel Peace Prize along with countless honorary degrees and more distinguished medals than she herself bothered to count. She had amassed millions of dollars (all of which she gave to the poor). Yet despite all the accolades showered upon her, she said she was only "a little pencil" in God's hand.[11]

In radical contrast to the self-centered pride underpinning the old feminism, Mother Teresa's attitude of humility was never more embodied than on the night she addressed about one thousand U.N. diplomats and dignitaries, most of them dressed in black ties and evening gowns. What did she do that October day before she rode in an unimpressive old car to the U.N. and received a standing ovation? She went to Mass, spent an hour in Adoration, washed her sari, and cleaned the toilets.[12] Never one to be hung up on the tasks she was called to *do*, the saint focused only on each little duty as it was presented to her. She focused not on the importance of the tasks she *did* but only on who she and others *are* as children of God.

This is a radically upside-down way of thinking, far from the way the old 1960s power feminists taught women to think and the way I once thought when I was writing for women's magazines. I do not think it an exaggeration to suggest that every power feminist would like to be Mother Teresa when she's winning the Nobel Prize and receiving a standing ovation at the U.N. But few if any of them want to be Mother Teresa when she's picking lice off the poor and cleaning the toilets. Yet in the Christian worldview, the smallest, humblest task done in love for the glory of God is infinitely and eternally more important than the largest achievement done solely in pride for one's own goals and personal glory.

Further, who knows? In the eyes of the Father, the Son, and the Holy Spirit, the saint may have received more grace for just one humble little task she did than for all the seemingly much more important ones. As Saint John of the Cross says, "More pleasing to God is one good work, however small it be, that is done in secret with no desire that it shall be known than a thousand that are done with the desire that they may be known of men."[13] We often think we have to do something *big* to please God (he who has *already* changed the world). But, in reality, it's the *little* things that count. After all, the Almighty God is not impressed by human accomplishments. The Son voluntarily entered into this world from timelessness into time as a poor, helpless, little baby in a manger, not as a rich and powerful emperor in a palace.

Mother Teresa's dignity was not lowered when she was cleaning the toilets. Nor was her dignity elevated when she was accepting the Nobel Prize. She always remained aware that her dignity came from her ever-present identity as a beloved daughter of God, which led to her doing everything not for herself alone but for others and the glory of God. When the Nobel Prize committee wanted to throw an expensive dinner in her honor, Mother Teresa cheerfully declined the dinner and suggested they take the money they would have spent and give it to the poor.

Peculiar as it may seem to old-fashioned feminists of my boomer generation who used our time and spent much of our lives seeking *self-centered* power, the *self-giving* path of love that Mother Teresa followed is the path to *true* power. The general secretary of the U.N. himself—a man who could certainly recognize power when he saw it—called her "the most powerful woman in the world." There's illusionary, transitory power idolized (and often generated) by the media fantasy world—the kind Helen Gurley Brown and Kate Millett spent their lives attempting to acquire (and the kind that I, as an old-fashioned feminist, spent most of *my* life attempting to acquire). Then there's *real*, authentic power that comes from the true Spirit of God acting through his creatures—and a vast chasm lies between the two. We must keep the distinction between the two types of power foremost in our minds if we're to discern what's true in our lives and not be deceived by illusions.

Every power feminist alive would like to be Alice Paul when she's being applauded, toasted, and given awards for her work to win women the right to vote. But no power feminist wants to be Alice Paul when she's praying and fasting, imprisoned in solitary in a filthy workhouse, given worm-invested sour soup to eat, and gagging on a pipe rammed down her throat. Let's get real. Wars for women's dignity are won not by prancing around Washington, D.C., with a pink pussyhat on your head but by going to the mat and laying down your life to suffer for your convictions.

When Mother Teresa was once asked what she thought about feminism, she replied she didn't think about it: she was too busy taking care of the poor. And yet in her petite frame with her smiling face, she embodied everything the old feminists were secretly seeking: mission, purpose of life, joy, wholeness of personhood, even fame and power (which she completely ignored). In her motherly love for every person she met in the human family, armed with the confident strength born only from love for God and neighbor, she completely rose above what the world calls "feminism." One of her dearest friends, Saint John Paul II, called upon Christian women to create a "new feminism,"[14] and I think I would not be too far off the mark to believe he was suggesting we take saintly women like Mother Teresa of Calcutta as our role models.

Although Mother Teresa firmly defended all human life from the moment of conception, "less well publicized, but no less genuine, was [her] loving concern for those women who suffered under the burden of a past abortion," recalled Monsignor Leo Maasburg, who for many years served as the saint's spiritual adviser and confessor. "Such women belonged to a little circle of privileged persons whom Mother Teresa embraced with heartfelt love and in a special way." The monsignor recalled seeing "many young women with tear-stained faces who, after a meeting with Mother Teresa, were once again each able to trust in the love and forgiveness of God that Mother Teresa had just shown her so tangibly; it is that kind of love that restores people's hope of reconciliation and of being able to lead a happy life again." Although for Mother Teresa, the sanctity of a child's life "was absolutely inviolable and must be defended in every situation ... she also understood people's material and social needs, the abandonment and loneliness they feel in those difficult moments when they make their decision. She always had an open mind, open arms, and a wide-open heart for the victims of this spiritual dilemma."[15]

Happily, for every Saint Teresa of Calcutta who gains international acclaim for her sanctity and charitable good works, there are millions of strong, unknown soldiers like Margot, who showed me for the first time in my life what one faithful woman can accomplish with God's grace.

8

A HIDDEN ARMY OF LOVE

When the NOW members in the Chinese Room created a Bill of Rights that focused almost exclusively on sexual, economic, and political power, they overlooked the essential element we all need to be free: the power of God's love.

As a self-proclaimed secular humanist, Betty Friedan never articulated this higher truth. The essential primacy of God's love for human flourishing was not on her radar. But she did recognize the importance of human love. When speaking to the *Christian Science Monitor* about her book *The Second Stage* (published in 1981), Betty said this: "The women's movement as we know it has come to a dead-end. The women's movement did not fail in the battle for equality. Our failure was our blind spot about the family."[1] Speaking for herself and other founding mothers of NOW, Betty wrote: "For us, equality and the personhood of women never meant destruction of the family, repudiation of marriage or motherhood, or implacable sexual war with men."

She said the "new feminism" (which she called "the second stage") "involves coming to new terms with the family—new terms with love and with work,"[2] and, furthermore, this new stage of freedom "may not even be a women's movement. Men may be at the cutting edge of the second stage."[3] In fact, she added, "I think ... that the women's movement has come just about as far as it can in terms of women alone."[4]

Nor did the mother of the 1960s women's movement see a woman simply as a man with female genitalia, as the editors of *Glamour* magazine apparently did when they proclaimed transgender Bruce (Caitlyn) Jenner to be their 2015 "Woman of the Year." Rather, Betty called upon feminists to affirm the *differences* between men and women. Condemning the fact that some feminists "denied real differences between women and men except for the sex organs themselves," she wrote, they "still do not understand that true equality is not possible unless those differences between men and women are affirmed."[5]

I was amazed when I came upon this statement because ... well, you know, the pope could have said that.

Rebuilding America

"Never doubt that a small group of thoughtful, committed citizens can change the world," anthropologist Margaret Mead reportedly said. "Indeed, it's the only thing that ever has."[6] In my travels around the country, I've met such small, dedicated groups of pro-life people in Omaha, Cleveland, Kansas City, San Diego, San Francisco, Austin, Indianapolis, Cleveland, Baltimore, Albuquerque, Orlando, Boston, Washington, D.C., and Manchester, New Hampshire, to name only some of the places I've visited. They're everywhere. They're raising smart, strong boys and girls, teaching sixth grade, working in pregnancy centers, protesting domestic violence, rescuing victims of sex-trafficking, answering crisis hotlines, adopting foster kids, praying before Planned Parenthood clinics, helping pregnant women finish college, fighting pornography, caring for the sick and the elderly, lobbying state and national legislators, working as pro-life doctors, nurses, lawyers, artists, writers, bakers, florists, photographers, filmmakers, and entrepreneurs ... the list goes on and on.

They're not striving to be superstars or earn millions of dollars (although some of them have done both). Rather, these people of faith are quietly working to love and nurture their families, communities, and others (even those who hate them) one small step and one day at a time. I am firmly convinced, more convinced than I have ever been of anything in my life, that these courageous women and the men who stand with them represent *the authentic feminist movement of the twenty-first century*. This vast network woven of love for God and others extends throughout our nation and includes (but is not in the least limited to) many people who work with the National Right to Life Committee (1968), Feminists for Life (1972), Birthright (1968), Americans United for Life (1971), March for Life (1973), Care Net (1975), American Family Association (1977), Students for Life of America (under another name, 1977), Concerned Women for America (1979), American Life League (1979), Pro-Life Action League (1980), Human Life International (1981), Anglicans for Life (incorporated in 1983), Priests for Life (1990), Susan B. Anthony List (1993), Vision America (1994), The Center for Family and Human Rights (1997), Endow (2003), Live Action (2003), 40 Days for Life (2004), Walk for Life West Coast (2005), Jewish Pro-Life Foundation (2006), National Black Pro-Life Coalition (2011), Women Speak for Themselves (2012), and umpteen state and local groups. This doesn't begin to include the many powerful professional groups that continually fight for life, such as the Thomas More Law Center, Legatus, Physicians for Life, Catholic

Medical Association, Alliance Defending Freedom, the Becket Fund for Religious Liberty, and many others too numerous to list here.

Please don't get me wrong. I'm not saying pro-life feminists are lifting America up by focusing on political action alone or by identifying with a particular political party. As Christians, we are called to achieve a reasonable balance between prayer and action. On the one hand, as Pope Benedict XVI reminded us, "The legitimate separation of church and state cannot be taken to mean that the church must be silent on certain issues, nor that the state may choose not to engage, or be engaged by, the voices of committed believers in determining the values which will shape the future of the nation."[7]

On the other hand, anytime we put "political activism" (or any other false idol) first and Christ second, we will likely do little good. For Christ tells us, "Apart from me, you can do nothing" (Jn 15:5). By listening to God in prayer, and then doing what He tells them to do, pro-life feminists are offering what Pope Benedict XVI said that the Church offers: "a life choice that goes beyond the political sphere."[8] The old feminism was all about sex, politics, and power, which naturally spawned a lot of anger. The new feminism transcends politics and is about the self-giving love that transfigures the world.

Many of the pro-life women and men I've met, those I think of as the honorable old guard, have been fighting for the family and the wholeness of a woman's personhood for more than fifty years. Truly independent in their thinking and able to move beyond cultural and historical limitations, they've refused to buy into the lies the media world of fantasy keeps spinning. Some have been martyrs for the truth. They've been arrested, indicted, and had their livelihoods destroyed. Yet despite the overwhelming odds working against them, these strong-minded women and men of character have not given up hope. I've met them face-to-face. They pray fervently, they love deeply, they never quit. And that's why I'm convinced they're unstoppable.

Propaganda and the Media Fantasy World

If pro-life feminists (those standing up and speaking out for women's true dignity) are everywhere, why haven't we heard more about them? For one simple reason: because media people like me, locked tightly inside our culture's little ideological boxes, *simply cannot see them.* By 1979, Judge Noonan wrote, almost everyone in the mass media was pro-abortion: "Virtually every major newspaper in the country was on [the pro-abortion] side, as were the radio stations, the news commentators, the disc jockeys, the pollsters, the syndicated columnists, the editorial writers, the reporters, the news services, the journals of information and the journals of public opinion. With the notable exception of three or four syndicated writers" (including William Buckley and George Will) and the single exception of the *National Review,* "every major molder of public opinion in the press" remained pro-abortion or indifferent to the issue.[9]

If feminism means primarily one thing to you—the "right" to abortion—then, strange as it may sound, you literally *cannot see* hundreds of thousands of pro-life feminists marching before your very eyes. Their true significance escapes you. They just look like weirdoes to you, strange warriors from an alien planet who are best vilified or ignored.

"The face of the pro-life movement is a young woman's face,"[10] says Kristan Hawkins, president of Students for Life of America, which now has pro-life groups on over eight hundred school campuses in America. Yet even though the pro-life feminist movement has long been gaining momentum, Hawkins observes that many reporters simply can't see the truth before their very eyes. When an ABC reporter, who obviously favored abortion, followed Kristan around campus for a story, the question the reporter kept coming back to was: "There are all these intelligent, young, attractive women in your group. Where did they all come from?"[11] One can only shudder at the words of Malcolm Muggeridge, who observed, "King Herod has always had a bad press for slaughtering the innocents, but ... nowadays a good campaign on the media for legalized abortion will facilitate the slaughter of millions on the highest humanitarian principles before they are even born."[12]

The fiercest battle of our time is the battle for the human mind. Propaganda, with its tendency to twist words, polarize debates, and create divisions, is designed to trap our thoughts and make our minds its prisoner. In fact, I would suggest that whenever you see an intensely polarized debate in the news, you can bet propaganda is at work, and the whole truth lies somewhere between the two extremes.

Journalists like me who consider themselves "well-informed" may, in fact, be the most vulnerable of all to polarizing propaganda. Why? Jacques Ellul offered three reasons: (1) We absorb the most massive amounts of secondhand, unverifiable information; (2) we feel a compelling need to have an opinion on every important issue of the day (and it's therefore easy for us to succumb to opinions offered to us by clever propagandists); and (3) we consider ourselves capable of "judging for ourselves," so we imagine ourselves to be immune to propaganda. We think somehow the propagandist's highly sophisticated tools of persuasion won't work on us, because we proudly believe we're too intelligent to be taken in.

Further, propaganda keeps people like me from having a divided heart: it wards off internal conflict. As Ellul points out, we all have a great need for "self-justification." Taking abortion again as a benchmark, I would suspect just from my own personal experience that many female journalists have had abortions (as I did)[*] and many male journalists have encouraged their girlfriends and wives to have abortions. So not only do journalists believe the propaganda that sexualized feminism is good for a woman, but they also *need* to believe the slogans to self-justify the painful, antiwoman choices they've made in their lives. Propaganda "eliminates inner conflicts, tensions, self-criticism and doubt," Ellul explains.[13] It provides pat rationalizations not only for past actions but for future actions as well.

Shattering the Darkness

And yet, occasionally, the light shines out of the darkness, and a slender beam of truth breaks through. On September 14, 1979, speaker Michael Harrington (a Catholic-turned-atheist who had worked with Catholic social activist Dorothy Day) shocked a well-heeled Planned Parenthood gathering at Rockefeller University when he stated what I, too, have seen: he said that his travels around the U.S. had convinced him the right-to-life movement was "one of the few genuine social movements of the

---

[*]Suffice it to say, it was the worst, most destructive decision of my life. Abortion is an irreversible decision made in the blink of an eye, under pressure and fear, with consequences that last a lifetime.

1970s." Referring to the pro-life movement's success "in capturing an ideal and mobilizing people in support of it," Harrington called the new pro-life feminism "the anti-women's movement women's movement."[14]

"If the tone of the evening was any indication," the *New York Times* reported, pro-abortion factions "are worried that their own movement lacks that kind of vitality."[15] Already by 1979, NOW had one hundred thousand members[16] ... and the National Right to Life Committee alone had 110 times that many—*eleven million* members.[17]

What's more, this grassroots movement has only gotten stronger—and younger. In 2010 when she was still president of NARAL, Democratic Party operative Nancy Keenan arrived at Washington, D.C.'s Union Station on January 22, the day thousands of young people were pouring into the city from all over the nation for the annual March for Life. "I just thought, my gosh, they are so young," Keenan told *Newsweek.* "There are so many of them, and they are so young."[18] In one of its own polls, NARAL itself found a significant "intensity gap" among the young on the abortion issue. Among Americans under age thirty, 51 percent of pro-lifers—compared to 26 percent of abortion-rights supporters—considered abortion a "very important" voting issue.[19]

As you may recall from chapter 5, in the 1976 presidential campaign, opinion polls showed a bare 1 percent of the public considered abortion a national election issue.[20] By the election of 2016 (the first year I spoke at the March for Life), the number of registered voters who considered abortion a "top issue" had shot up to 45 percent.[21]

Power in a democracy doesn't come from the top down, or at least it shouldn't. If a democracy is working properly, power grows from the ground up. Although the deep-pockets media never tell you this, the pro-life feminist movement had grassroots power in 1979, and it still has this grassroots power today.

In fact, from what I've observed during my travels around the country, I think it's safe to say that the old pro-abortion feminist movement at this point in history is no longer a viable woman's movement. Rather, the old media-anointed, pro-abortion feminism that emerged in 1967 from the Chinese Room is now—and perhaps to some extent always has been—primarily a movement financed largely by the abortion and contraception industries and their supporters, and it is being propped up and maintained only by mountainous reams of propaganda being beamed 24/7/365 at mainstream media reporters, who then dutifully pass it on to a slumbering American public (who may at last slowly be waking up).

As a journalist, I'm convinced one way to wake them up faster, and to keep more women and girls from being hurt, is for pro-life feminists to take back the F-word and shout it to the skies.

POSTSCRIPT

Our whole nation is fighting over what it means to be human. At its very foundation, "What does it mean to be a person?" is the existential question that lies hidden at the heart of our so-called culture wars.

If we are *not* made in the image of God and if we are *not* made for eternal happiness—if we are just sophisticated animals meant to consume as much stuff as possible and to have as much pleasure as we can before we die—then there's no reason why we can't kill babies in the womb and sell off their body parts for profit. If we're just sophisticated animals, a baby is little more than a chicken or a lamb, and the U.S. Supreme Court's *Roe v. Wade* decision is defensible and valid.

Likewise, if God did *not* create us as man *and* woman, if we create ourselves and choose our sexual identities in any way that strikes our fancy (as Kinsey claimed), then the *Obergefell v. Hodges* decision giving same-sex couples the "right to marry" is also defensible and valid. If a human being is only a sophisticated sexual animal, then what's wrong with *Playboy*? What's wrong with pornography? What's wrong with sex trafficking? What's wrong with sexual abuse of children? What's wrong with sleeping with your married boss and destroying his family? If there is no eternal life in Christ and He is not risen from the dead, then the material world isn't sacred and our time on this earth means nothing. So, why doesn't everyone just relax and have fun?

As Dostoevsky's character Ivan famously put it in *The Brothers Karamazov*, if God does not exist, then everything is permitted. If there is no God, then there are no rules to live by, no moral law we must follow; we can do whatever we want.

And yet despite the Kinsey-*Playboy-Cosmo-Sexual Politics* reduction of a woman to a sexual animal, the outrage sparked by the #MeToo Movement plainly shows the vast majority of Americans still believe a woman is much *more* than an animal: she's a human *person* and she deserves our respect. Although our culture permits and even celebrates all sorts of visual exploitation that treats women as sexual animals in our media, all people of goodwill suddenly draw the line when a woman speaks up and says she's been harassed, abused, or raped. The ability to speak in defense of one's dignity is a human trait. Animals don't intellectually speak up to defend themselves.

When we, as Americans, pledge we are "*one* nation, under God, *indivisible*, with liberty and justice for *all*," we are declaring the divine truth that we as a people are all interconnected in one human family. We believe in liberty and justice for *all*, the smallest and weakest as well as the strongest. Human rights are not isolated, private, and at war. *Human rights are indivisible.* We can't hurt the unborn baby without hurting the mother. We can't hurt the mother without hurting the baby. And we can't hurt either of them without hurting us all.

That said, let's look at this story one more time and recap what we've seen. What actually happened? What does it mean? And what can we do?

First and foremost, we must silence our minds and hearts, pray, and *listen*. Whatever injustices we may be called to fight, we cannot fight them alone, because we are *not* alone. If we're willing to welcome him into our hearts,

God is with us. "First learn to pray. Then you will easily perform all your good works," a monk once told me, and he's right. What can you do? Your most powerful weapons are prayer and fasting. Pray and fast, and you will find that God will lead you to know what action to take; then take the action.

Second, as the pro-life, pro-family, pro-*personhood* branch of the women's movement, we need to reclaim our true history and tell our story, which has not been synthesized until now. We need to name, claim, and proclaim that *we*—not Planned Parenthood, not the National Organization for Women, not NARAL Pro-Choice America—are the ones who can speak most clearly for the authentic dignity and respect of all women and girls around the world, and it is our deeper understanding of a woman's personhood that can purify and therefore represent the more genuine, authentic feminism of the twenty-first century.

We also need to separate true feminism from the sexual revolution in our own minds and in the minds of others. True family feminism seeks to enhance women's dignity and freedom, including the right to be respected and admired for choosing to be a stay-at-home mom. The feminism that was secretly hijacked by sexual-revolution forces in the Chinese Room separates women from men and children, creates gender confusion, and turns women's bodies into commodities. It has created a multibillion-dollar porn industry, wrecked romance, created a divorce culture, and left millions of single mothers struggling in poverty to raise children alone. This is not freedom. It's a form of bondage, a betrayal of women, motherhood, childhood, fatherhood, and the family.

Third, we need to stop being bamboozled by the media. Despite everything I've said in this book about the media, I still have a great love and respect for the fourth estate. Without a professional corps of honest journalists working hard to sort out the truth and do their jobs well, our democracy cannot survive. This is not the time to hate the media or to dismiss everything we see or read as "fake news." Rather, we need to recognize the value—and limitations—of the media, to take what good we can out of what we're given while being aware of the vested political and economic interests that lurk behind many of the stories we read, and to remain skeptical about stories that seem a little "too pat."

Malcolm Muggeridge knew all about the media fantasy world we've been talking about because, like me, he had personally witnessed it for decades from the inside. Toward the end of his life, after a long illustrious career, Muggeridge said this: "I am more convinced than of anything else that I have ever thought, or considered, or believed, that the only antidote to the media's world of fantasy is the reality of Christ's Kingdom proclaimed in the New Testament."[1] I agree with Muggeridge completely.

As a journalist, I was deceived, but the grassroots workers were not deceived. They're the real unsung heroes of this story. Pope Saint John Paul II called upon Christians to create a "new feminism," and I believe those in the pro-life movement are already doing exactly that.

When I tell people how this whole feminist mess began, they frequently ask: "Is there any hope?" Of course there is hope. Larry Lader thought he had won the abortion wars the day he convinced Betty Friedan to include abortion in NOW's political "Bill of Rights" and the U.S. Supreme Court went on to legalize abortion in all fifty states. But through the beautiful pro-life women's movement, God has kept abortion and other personhood issues alive across this nation for the past fifty years. They say the devil never sleeps. Well, pro-life feminists don't sleep either.

As we have seen throughout this book, people long dead have shaped many Americans' thinking. But their thoughts do not have to be our thoughts. We, the living, can reconsider and correct the errors made by previous generations. In hope and love, with God's grace, we can think things through afresh and begin anew.

So let us not despair to be living at a time when we're surrounded by so much violence and so many problems. For the stock market may collapse, institutions may crumble, tyrants may fall, but the dignity and wholeness of the human person established by and revealed in Jesus Christ will never pass away.

Yes, you'll have political setbacks. Yes, you'll continue to win some battles and lose others. But I always remember what Saint Teresa of Calcutta (a true contemplative in the world) said one day when she attended a congressional reception on Capitol Hill. A senator complimented her, saying, "Mother, you're doing marvelous work." She humbly replied, "It's God's work." He then asked, "But in India, where there are so many problems, can you ever be successful at what you do—isn't it hopeless to try?" And she replied, "Well, Senator, we're not always called to be successful, but we're always called to be faithful."[2]

For over a century, from the days of Alice Paul, generations of steadfast souls in the pro-life women's movement in America have been faithful. Their contribution to history has been largely ignored, but it will not be forgotten. A massive army of young women and men have now seized the pro-life banner, lifting it high, carrying it forward into tomorrow. And there should be no doubt in anyone's mind that if you keep listening to God in prayer and acting on what you hear Him lovingly say, your particular, irreplaceable contribution to this spiritual battle *will* make a difference. In the inspiring words of Saint John Henry Newman, God has a good for you to accomplish and He will not cast you aside.

What are *you* going to do?

ACKNOWLEDGMENTS

Although a writer spends many hours in silent solitude, no book is ever written alone. I have been blessed to receive invaluable help, encouragement, and love from many friends, family members, neighbors, and colleagues, far more than I can mention here. Those who deserve special mention, in no particular order, include Mark and Stephanie Rohloff, Nathaniel and Alysa Slinkert, Joanna Slinkert, Jo Torreano, Margaret Manion, Margaret and Paul Turano, Mike and Robin Carter, Leslie Smyth, Michael and Christina Turano, Philip Gilbert, Jim King, Mary Davenport, Kelsey Bolar, Lauren Evans, Lila Rose, and all the brilliant, talented, and loving people at Ignatius Press and the Augustine Institute, including Father Joseph Fessio, Joseph Pearce, Mark Brumley, Diane Eriksen, Grace Hagan, Darlene Broussard, Laura Peredo, Ben Dybas, and Christina Gray.

A special thank-you goes to Liz Mullen and Sue Jones for believing in this book from the beginning and for offering their unwavering friendship and brilliant editorial advice during the long process, even before the book was sent to a publisher.

It gives me special joy to thank Father David Anderson, who frequently told me not to write this book and yet continually supported me with his fervent faith and constant prayers. I can't thank this good priest enough for his steadfast guidance and for the many important things I've learned from him.

Last but far from least, a heartfelt gift of gratitude goes to my son Dustin and my daughter-in-law Jen for their indispensable support and for urging me to write the book I'd long been wanting to write.

NOTES

Introduction: It's Time to Reclaim Feminism

1. John Paul II, *Evangelium Vitae* (March 25, 1995), no. 99, http://www.vatican.va/content/john-paul-ii/en/encyclicals/documents/hf_jp-ii_enc_25031995_evangelium-vitae.html.

2. "Pope John Paul II: The Feminist Pope," USCCB (blog), April 18, 2011, https://usccbmedia.blogspot.com/2011/04/pope-john-paul-ii-feminist-pope.html.

3. *Ordinatio Sacerdotalis*, Apostolic Letter of John Paul II to the Bishops of the Catholic Church on Reserving Priestly Ordination to Men Alone (May 22, 1994), http://w2.vatican.va/content/john-paul-ii/en/apost_letters/1994/documents/hf_jp-ii_apl_19940522_ordinatio-sacerdotalis.html.

4. Donna Jackson, *How to Make the World a Better Place for Women in Five Minutes a Day* (New York: Hyperion, 1992). I researched and ghostwrote about one-third of this book; my name was in the acknowledgments but not on the cover.

5. See Marcia Cohen, epilogue of *The Sisterhood: The Inside Story of the Women's Movement and the Leaders Who Made It Happen* (New York: Fawcett Columbine, 1988), 359–79, in which everyone from Gloria Steinem to Susan Brownmiller spoke of "the end of the movement".

6. Natalie Angier, "The Origin, Procreation, and Hopes of an Angry Feminist," in *The Bitch in the House*, ed. Cathi Hanauer (New York: HarperCollins, 2003), 220.

Chapter 1: Remembering Our Story

1. Donald Calloway, M.I.C., *Under the Mantle: Marian Thoughts from a 21st Century Priest* (Stockbridge, MA: Marian Press, 2013), 263.

2. Malcolm Muggeridge, *The End of Christendom—But Not of Christ* (Grand Rapids, MI: Eerdman's, 1980), 38.

3. Robert S. Gallagher, "Alice Paul: 'I Was Arrested, Of Course ...,'" *American Heritage* 25, no. 2 (February 1974), https://www.american heritage.com/alice-paul-i-was-arrested-course.

4. Doris Stevens, *Jailed for Freedom* (New York: Boni & Liveright, 1920), 16.

5. Ibid., 28.

6. Ibid., 108.

7. Ibid., 142.

8. Ibid., 356.

9. Ibid., 115.

10. bid., 188–89.

11. Ibid., 153.

12. Ibid., 226.

13. Ibid., 16.

14. Mary Krane Derr, Rachel MacNair, and Linda Naranjo-Huebl, *ProLife Feminism: Yesterday and Today*, expanded 2nd ed. (Kansas City, MO: Feminism and Nonviolence Studies Association, 2005), 172. Originally from Evelyn K. Samras Judge's letters to Mary Krane Derr, September 12 and 21, 1989; archived at Feminists for Life of America, Alexandria, VA. (Judge was Paul's colleague from the 1940s on.)

15. Cynthia Harrison, *On Account of Sex: The Politics of Women's Issues, 1945–1968* (Berkeley: University of California Press, 1988), 205.

16. See also Cindy Osborne, "Pat Goltz, Catherine Callaghan, and the Founding of Feminists for Life," in Derr, MacNair, and Naranjo-Huebl, *ProLife Feminism*, 223–24. Paul's views on abortion are also documented in Alice Paul and Amelia R. Fry, *Conversations with Alice Paul: Woman Suffrage and the Equal Rights Amendment: Oral History Transcript/ and Related Material, 1972–1976* (Charleston, NC: Nabu Press, 2010).

17. As journalist George Gilder observed, "Essentially, the ERA would have granted to the federal bench, long dominated below the Supreme Court level by the some 400 liberal appointees of the Carter Administration, nearly carte blanche to redefine the relations between the sexes in America. Voluminous testimony before Senator Orrin Hatch's subcommittee of the Judiciary Committee showed that, among many other significant effects, the Amendment would likely have: 1) eliminated all rights of wives and mothers to be supported by their husbands, except to the extent husbands could claim an equal right; 2) eliminated all laws in any way restricting the rights of the gay liberation movement publicly to teach, proselytize, or practice their sexual ideology; 3) forced sexual integration of all schools,

clubs, colleges, athletic teams, and facilities; 4) forced the drafting of women and the sexual integration of all military units; 5) threatened the tax exemption of most religious schools; and 6) compelled the use of government funds for abortions" (George Gilder, *Men and Marriage* [Gretna, LA: Pelican Publishing, 1992], 103–4). Gilder wrote those words in 1973 (*Men and Marriage* was previously entitled *Sexual Suicide*, published in 1973). Despite the defeat of the ERA, nearly all of these predictions have now been written into our nation's laws by legislators and the courts.

18. Joseph W. Dellapenna, *Dispelling the Myths of Abortion History* (Durham, NC: Carolina Academic Press, 2006), 387.

19. Ibid., 387–88.

20. Frederica Mathewes-Green, "The Bitter Price of 'Choice,'" in *Prolife Feminism: Yesterday and Today*, ed. Mary Krane Derr, Rachel MacNair, and Linda Naranjo-Huebl (New York: Sulzburger & Graham, 1995), 183.

21. A private, upscale women's college, Smith boasts many famous graduates, including Anne Morrow Lindberg, Nancy Reagan, Barbara Bush, and Julie Nixon Eisenhower.

22. Betty Friedan, *The Feminine Mystique* (New York: Norton, 2001), 15.

23. Edith Stein, *Essays on Woman*, Collected Works of Edith Stein (Washington, DC: ICS Publications, 1987), 2:92–93.

24. Alexander Elchaninov, *The Diary of a Russian Priest* (Crestwood, NY: St. Vladimir's Seminary Press, 1967), 34.

25. Friedan, *Feminine Mystique*, 344.

26. Betty Friedan, *The Second Stage* (New York: Dell, 1991), 305.

27. Karol Wojtyla, *Love and Responsibility* (Boston: Pauline Books & Media, 2013), 5.

28. Paul Vitz, *Psychology as Religion: The Cult of Self-Worship* (Grand Rapids, MI: Eerdmans, 1977).

29. Friedan, *Feminine Mystique*, 386.

30. Saint Gregory of Nyssa, Letters, Complete, 2. Available online at https://www.elpenor.org/nyssa/letters.asp?pg=2.

31. *Love and Responsibility*, 4.

32. Viktor E. Frankl, *The Unconscious God* (New York: Pocket Books, 1975), 91.

33. Ibid., 139.

34. Betty Friedan, *Life So Far* (New York: Simon & Schuster, 2000), 200–201.

35. Ibid., 78.

36. David Sheff, "Playboy Interview: Betty Friedan," *Playboy*, September 1992, reprinted in *Interviews with Betty Friedan*, ed. Janann Sherman (Jackson: University Press of Mississippi, 2002), 108.

37. Michael Shelden, "Behind the Feminine Mystique," *London Daily Telegraph*, August 9, 1999; available in Sherman, *Interviews with Betty Friedan*, 191.

38. Zubeida Mustafa, "Still Talking, Writing and Connecting," *Dawn*, March 25, 2007.

39. Caroline Bird with Sara Welles Briller, *Born Female: The High Cost of Keeping Women Down* (New York: Pocket Books, 1969), 170.

40. Betty Friedan, *It Changed My Life: Writings on the Women's Movement* (New York: Random House, 1976), 305–6.

41. Ibid.

42. Carl Degler, *At Odds: Women and the Family in America from the Revolution to the Present* (Oxford, UK: Oxford University Press, 1980), 327.

Chapter 2: Woman as a Sexual Animal

1. Manford Kuhn, "Kinsey's View of Human Behavior," in *Sexual Behavior in American Society: An Appraisal of the First Two Kinsey Reports*, ed. Jerome Himelhoch and Sylvia Fleis Fava (New York: W. W. Norton, 1955), 34. This quote is from a paper published in the April 1954 issue of *Social Problems*, written by State University of Iowa sociologist Dr. Manford H. Kuhn.

2. James H. Jones, *Alfred C. Kinsey: A Public/Private Life* (New York: Norton, 1997), 684.

3. Ibid., 569.

4. Ibid., 586.

5. Ibid., 577.

6. Ibid.

7. Alfred Charles Kinsey, Wardell Baxter Pomeroy, Clyde Eugene Martin, *Sexual Behavior in the Human Female* (Philadelphia: W. B. Saunders, 1953), 53.

8. Ibid., 36.

9. Jones, *Alfred C. Kinsey*, 578–79. Original source: Geoffrey Gorer, "A Statistical Study of Sex," review in *New York Herald Tribune*, February 1, 1948, 4.

10. Geoffrey Gorer, "Nature, Science, and Dr. Kinsey," in Himelhoch and Fava, *Sexual Behavior in American Society*, 51. Kinsey, of course, was far from the only person to use "science" as propaganda. As Gabriele Kuby observed, "Since Marx's time, propaganda has wrapped itself in a cloak of 'science' and at the same time betrayed the very essence of science—the unbiased search for the truth. This high ideal is the basis for the unrivaled fruitfulness of Western science. If it goes down, science goes down with it and is reduced to being a servant for special interest groups" (Gabrielle Kuby, James Patrick Kirchner, and Robert Spaeman, *The Global Sexual Revolution: Destruction of Freedom in the Name of Freedom* [Kettering, OH: LifeSite, 2015], 36). Thanks to Kinsey and other researchers like him, in some pockets of science, particularly in the social sciences, this downfall of science has already happened.

11. George Simpson, "Nonsense about Women," *Humanist* 14 (March–April 1954): 49–56; reprinted with slight revisions in Himelhoch and Fava, *Sexual Behavior in American Society*, 64.

12. Ibid., 65.

13. Jones, *Alfred C. Kinsey*, 678.

14. Ibid., 579.

15. Daniel K. Williams, *Defenders of the Unborn: The Pro-Life Movement before Roe v. Wade* (New York: Oxford University Press, 2016), 180.

16. Jones, *Alfred C. Kinsey*, 678. "Misogyny" is the word that Jones uses, and it seems appropriate.

17. Kira Cochrane, "Is the Playboy Party Over?" *Guardian*, May 31, 2011, https://www.theguardian.com/lifeandstyle/2011/may/31/playboy-hugh-hefner-sexism.

18. David Sheff, "*Playboy* Interview: Betty Friedan," *Playboy*, September 1992, reprinted in *Interviews with Betty Friedan*, ed. Janann Sherman (Jackson: University Press of Mississippi, 2002), 91–92.

19. Marcia Cohen, *The Sisterhood: The Inside Story of the Women's Movement and the Leaders Who Made It Happen* (New York: Fawcett Columbine, 1988), 114.

Chapter 3: The Rule of Helen Gurley Brown

1. Chris Welles, "Helen Gurley Brown Turns Editor—Soaring Success of the Iron Butterfly," *Life*, November 19, 1965, 65–72.

2. *On Living Simply: The Golden Voice of John Chrysostom*, compiled by Robert Van de Weyer (Ligouri, MO: Ligouri/Triumph, 1996), 67.

3. Edward Bernays, *Propaganda* (Brooklyn, NY: IG Publishing, 1928), 77–78.

4. Michele Ingrassia, "Now, the Cosmo Baby," *Newsday*, August 20, 1986, 4.

5. Mildred Newman and Bernard Berkowitz, *How to Be Your Own Best Friend* (New York: Random House, 1971).

6. Jennifer Scanlon, *Bad Girls Go Everywhere: The Life of Helen Gurley Brown* (Oxford: Oxford University Press, 2009), 185. Originally from text of television show, July 24, 1991, from the Helen Gurley Brown Papers, housed in the Sophia Smith Collection at Smith College, Northampton, MA.

7. Ibid.

8. Jeffner Allen, "Motherhood: The Annihilation of Women," in *Mothering: Essays in Feminism Theory*, ed. Joyce Trebilcot (Totowa, NJ: Rowman & Allanheld, 1983), 315; see 315–30.

9. Ibid., 316.

10. Ibid., 317.

11. Helen Gurley Brown, "What to Wear to Be Especially Sexy," in *Sex and the Office* (New York: Barnes & Noble Books, 1964), 32–34.

12. Ibid., 33.

13. Ibid., 34.

14. Ibid., 184. This quote was so spicy—and guaranteed to sell books—that it was edited and placed on the back cover.

15. Helen Gurley Brown, "At Work, Sexual Electricity Sparks Creativity," *Wall Street Journal*, October 29, 1991.

16. Scanlon, *Bad Girls Go Everywhere*, 214.

17. Welles, "Helen Gurley Brown Turns Editor," 72.

18. Ibid.

19. Ibid.

20. Linda Charlton, "Women Seeking Equality March on 5th Avenue Today," *New York Times*, August 26, 1970, 44.

21. Ibid.

22. Brooke Hauser, *Enter Helen: The Invention of Helen Gurley Brown and the Rise of the Modern Single Woman* (New York: Harper, 2016), 325.

23. Ibid., 328.

24. Betty Friedan, *Life So Far* (New York: Simon & Schuster, 2000), 78.

25. Ema O'Connor, "How Anti-Abortion Advocates Are Using a Pro-Woman Message to Appeal to a New Generation," *BuzzFeed News*,

July 30, 2018, https://www.buzzfeednews.com/article/emaoconnor/how-advocates-are-using-feminist-language-to-rebrand-the.

Chapter 4: The Midnight Vote in the Chinese Room

1. Lawrence Lader, *Abortion II: Making the Revolution* (Boston: Beacon Press, 1973), viii.

2. Bernard Nathanson with Richard Ostling, *Aborting America* (Toronto: Life Cycle Books, 1979), 32.

3. Serrin Foster, "The Feminist Case against Abortion," in *The Cost of Choice: Women Evaluate the Impact of Abortion*, ed. Erika Bachiochi (San Francisco: Encounter, 2004), 33–38.

4. In her blurb, Friedan wrote, "Lawrence Lader's book is the first daring revelation of the cruelty and damage inflicted on American women by our antiquated abortion laws. It is not only an authoritative study of the hypocrisy and absurdity of abortion practices; it is a courageous blueprint of what women must do to abolish the state's power to force them to bear a child against their will." Authoritative? *Really?* Well, this blurb only goes to show that Friedan, brilliant as she was, was no more immune to propaganda than the rest of us are.

5. Lader, *Abortion II*, 18.

6. For a more complete story about how this happened, see my book *Subverted* (San Francisco: Ignatius Press, 2015), 89–97.

7. Lawrence Lader, *Ideas Triumphant: Strategies for Social Change and Progress* (Santa Ana, CA: Seven Locks Press, 2003), 79.

8. Ibid., 80.

9. Bernard Nathanson, "Confessions of an Ex-Abortionist," Catholic Education Resource Center, accessed December 3, 2019, https://www.catholiceducation.org/en/controversy/abortion/confessions-of-an-ex-abortionist.html.

10. Ibid.

11. Ibid.

12. Lawrence Lader, *Abortion* (New York: Bobbs-Merrill, 1966), 2.

13. C.S. Lewis, essay "Priestesses in the Church?" Originally published under the title "Notes on the Way," in *Time and Tide* 29 (August 14, 1948), available at http://www.episcopalnet.org/TRACTS/priestesses.html.

14. Betty Friedan, *Life So Far* (New York: Simon & Schuster, 2000), 204.

15. Judith Hole and Ellen Levine, *Rebirth of Feminism* (New York: Quadrangle Books, 1971), 439–40, appendix of historical documents.

16. Friedan, *Life So Far*, 206.

17. Martin Luther King Jr., "Transformed Nonconformist," in *A Gift of Love: Sermons from Strength to Love and Other Preaching* (Boston: Beacon Press, 2012), 13.

18. Betty Friedan, NOW press release regarding Second Annual National Conference, *Feminist Majority Foundation*, November 20, 1967, http://www.feminist.org/research/chronicles/early4.html.

19. "NOW Is Out of Kitchen—Stresses Abortion Reform," *Washington Post*, November 21, 1967, C1–C2.

Chapter 5: Beyond the Chinese Room

1. John T. Noonan Jr., *A Private Choice: Abortion in America in the Seventies* (New York: Free Press, 1979), 37.

2. Joseph W. Dellapenna, *Dispelling the Myths of Abortion History* (Durham, NC: Carolina Academic Press, 2006), 640.

3. Ibid. Originally from Andras Klinger, "Rapporteur's Summary: The World-Wide Problem of Abortion," *Proceedings of the Eighth International Conference of the International Planned Parenthood Federation* (London: International Planned Parenthood Federation, 1967), 153.

4. Alan F. Guttmacher, *Having a Baby* (New York: New American Library, 1947), 15.

5. Noonan, *Private Choice*, 37. Originally from Alan F. Guttmacher, *Birth Control and Love: The Complete Guide to Contraception and Fertility* (New York: Macmillan, 1961), 12.

6. Alan Guttmacher, "Symposium: Law, Morality, and Abortion," *Rutgers Law Review* 22 (1968): 415, 416.

7. Noonan, *Private Choice*, 37.

8. Mary Meehan, "ACLU v. Unborn Children," in *ProLife Feminism: Yesterday and Today*, expanded 2nd ed. (Kansas City, MO: Feminism and Nonviolence Studies Association, 2005), 367.

9. Ibid.

10. "Obstetricians Back Liberal Abortions," *New York Times*, May 10, 1968, 21.

11. "Report of the Chairman of the Executive Board of the American Public Health Association to the Governing Council, 1968," *American Journal of Public Health* (January 1969): 123–29.

12. Noonan, *Private Choice*, 70.

13. Linda Bird Francke, *The Ambivalence of Abortion* (New York: Random House, 1978), 243.

14. Andrea Dworkin, *Right-Wing Women* (New York: Perigee, 1983), 94–95.

15. "Neil Strauss Tells Emma Forrest 'All the Right Moves' for Bedding Ladies," *Guardian*, September 10, 2005. See also Suzanne Chazin, "Some Women Would Tell Eric Weber to Buzz Off, but Men Are Buying His Line on Picking Up Girls," *People Magazine*, August 17, 1981.

16. As a *Cosmopolitan* writer, I worked as a freelancer for Eric Weber on one of his later books, *The Divorced Woman's Guide to Meeting New Men: Where to Go and What to Do to Find Your Man* (New York: William Morrow, 1984). All the stories in the book on how to pick up men were, of course, fabricated.

17. Sue Browder, "Ah, Romance ... Where Has It Gone?", *Connecticut*, February 1985.

18. Judith Hole and Ellen Levine, *Rebirth of Feminism* (New York: Quadrangle Books, 1971), 96.

19. Judith Paterson, *Be Somebody: A Biography of Marguerite Rawalt* (Austin, TX: Eakin Press, 1986), 181.

20. Gail Collins, *When Everything Changed* (New York: Little, Brown, 2014), 235.

21. Hole and Levine, *Rebirth of Feminism*, 95–98; also author's phone interview with Patricia Bliss-Egan, Betty Boyer's niece, on March 19, 2013.

Chapter 6: Sexual Politics Enter the Fray

1. Lawrence Lader, *Ideas Triumphant: Strategies for Social Change and Progress* (Santa Ana, CA: Seven Locks Press, 2003), 106.

2. Betty Friedan, *It Changed My Life: Writings on the Women's Movement* (New York: Random House, 1976), 164.

3. Lader, *Ideas Triumphant*, 107.

4. "Who's Come a Long Way, Baby?", *Time*, August 31, 1970.

5. Kate Millett, *Sexual Politics* (London: Virago Press, 1977), 22.

6. Carol Adams, "The Book That Made Us Feminists," *New York Times*, September 7, 2017.

7. Susan Brownmiller, *In Our Time: Memoir of a Revolution* (New York: Dell, 1999), 148.

8. Adams, "Book That Made Us Feminists."

9. Kate Millett, *Mother Millett* (New York: Verso, 2001), 93.

10. Ibid., 27.

11. Ibid., 306.

12. Millett, *Sexual Politics*, 25.

13. Ronald V. Sampson, *The Psychology of Power* (New York: Vintage Books, 1968), 237.

14. Ibid. Original citation: Bertrand Russell, *Sceptical Essays* (New York: W. W. Norton, 1928), 118–19.

15. Sampson, *Psychology of Power*, 237.

16. Millett, *Sexual Politics*, 345.

17. Caryll Houselander, *The Reed of God* (Allen, TX: Christian Classics, 1987), 85.

18. Millett, *Sexual Politics*, 51.

19. F. J. Sheed, *Theology for Beginners* (Cincinnati, OH: Servant Books, 1981), 116.

20. Friedan, *It Changed My Life*, 161.

21. Millett, *Sexual Politics*, 22.

22. Friedan, *It Changed My Life*, 161.

23. Ibid., 162.

24. Ibid.

25. Ibid.

26. Millett, *Sexual Politics*, 34.

27. Ibid., 33.

28. Ibid., 168.

29. Ibid., 169.

30. Ibid., 176.

31. Ibid., 169.

32. Ibid.

33. Ibid., 169–70.

34. Virginia Rutter, "Bad Girl," *Psychology Today*, March–April 1994, 22.

35. Saint Gregory of Nyssa, Letters, Complete, 2. Available online at https://www.elpenor.org/nyssa/letters.asp?pg=2.

36. A Carthusian, *They Speak by Silences* (New York: Longmans, Green, 1955), 86.

37. Ibid., 92.

38. Thomas Merton, *Contemplative Prayer* (New York: Doubleday, 1971), 24.

39. Kate Millett, "The Feminist Time Forgot," *Guardian*, June 23, 1998.

40. Ibid.

41. Marcia Cohen, *The Sisterhood: The Inside Story of the Women's Movement and the Leaders Who Made It Happen* (New York: Fawcett Columbine, 1988), 254.

42. Joyce A. Martin et al., "Births: Final Data for 2017," National Vital Statistics Reports, vol. 67, no. 8 (Hyattsville, MD: National Center for Health Statistics, November 7, 2018).

Chapter 7: A New Hope Rises

1. Jennifer Scanlon, *Bad Girls Go Everywhere* (Oxford, UK: Oxford University Press, 2009), 188.

2. Ibid.

3. Myrna Blyth, *Spin Sisters: How the Women of the Media Sell Unhappiness—and Liberalism—to the Women of America* (New York: St. Martin's, 2004), ix.

4. Ibid., 273.

5. Margot Sheahan, *The Whole Parent: 12 Steps to Serenity for Unwed Parents* (Los Angeles: VCA Publishing, 2001), xv.

6. Ibid., xvi–xvii.

7. Ibid., xvii.

8. Ibid., 107.

9. Raoul Plus, S.J., *Radiating Christ* (Oak Lawn, IL: CMJ Marian Publishers, 1998), 60.

10. Leo Maasburg, *Mother Teresa of Calcutta: A Personal Portrait* (San Francisco: Ignatius Press, 2011), 175.

11. Mother Teresa, *No Greater Love* (Novato, CA: New World Library, 2002), 53.

12. Maasburg, *Mother Teresa*, 175.

13. John of the Cross, *Spiritual Sentences and Maxims*, 20, 2, in *The Complete Works of Saint John of the Cross*, vol. 2, trans. E. Allison Peers (Westminster, MD: Newman Press, 1949), 243.

14. John Paul II, *Evangelium Vitae* (March 25, 1995), no. 99, http://www.vatican.va/content/john-paul-ii/en/encyclicals/documents/hf_jp-ii_enc_25031995_evangelium-vitae.html.

15. Maasburg, *Mother Teresa*, 171–72.

Chapter 8: A Hidden Army of Love

1. Pamela Marsh, "Betty Friedan Calls for Less Abrasiveness, More Emphasis on the Family," *Christian Science Monitor*, October 28, 1981.

2. Betty Friedan, *The Second Stage* (New York: Dell, 1991), 16.

3. Marsh, "Betty Friedan Calls for Less Abrasiveness," 16.

4. Ibid., 15.

5. Friedan, *Second Stage*, 352.

6. Nancy C. Lutkehaus, *Margaret Mead: The Making of an American Icon* (Princeton, NJ: Princeton University Press, 2008), 261.

7. Alessandro Speciale, "Benedict Gives Direction to U.S. Bishops on Hot-Button Issues," *Religion News Service*, May 22, 2012, https://religionnews.com/2012/05/22/pope-benedict-xvi-gives-direction-to-u-s-bishops-on-hot-button-issues/.

8. Address of His Holiness Benedict XVI, Inaugural Session of the Fifth General Conference of the Bishops of Latin America and the Caribbean (May 13, 2007), http://www.vatican.va/content/benedict-xvi/en/speeches/2007/may/documents/hf_ben-xvi_spe_20070513_conference-aparecida.html.

9. John T. Noonan Jr., *A Private Choice: Abortion in America in the Seventies* (New York: Free Press, 1979), 69–70.

10. Sue Ellen Browder, "Women Betrayed: A New Generation Rallies Nationwide to Protest Planned Parenthood," *National Catholic Register*, July 31, 2015.

11. Ibid.

12. Malcolm Muggeridge, *Christ and the Media* (Vancouver, B.C.: Regent College Publishing, 2003), 15–16.

13. Jacques Ellul, *Propaganda: The Formation of Men's Attitudes* (New York: Vintage, 1965), 165.

14. Ann Crittenden, "A Colloquy on the Sanger Spirit," *New York Times*, September 18, 1979.

15. Ibid.

16. "Feminist Chronicles—1979," Feminist Majority Foundation, 2014, http://www.feminist.org/research/chronicles/fc1979.html.

17. Gail Collins, *When Everything Changed: The Amazing Journey of American Women from 1960 to the Present* (New York: Little, Brown, 2009), 234.

18. Sarah Kliff, "Why Young Voters Are Lukewarm on Abortion Rights," *Newsweek*, April 15, 2010, http://www.newsweek.com/why-young-voters-are-lukewarm-abortion-rights-70311.

19. Ibid.

20. Linda Bird Francke, *The Ambivalence of Abortion* (New York: Random House, 1978), 243.

21. "Top Voting Issues in 2016 Election," Pew Research Center, July 7, 2016, https://www.people-press.org/2016/07/07/4-top-voting-issues-in-2016-election/.

Postscript

1. Malcolm Muggeridge, *Christ and the Media* (Vancouver, B.C.: Regent College Publishing, 2003), 24.

2. Mother Teresa, *A Simple Path*, compiled by Lucinda Vardey (New York: Ballantine Books, 1995), 152–53.